A CHRISTIAN ENDING

A CHRISTIAN ENDING

A HANDBOOK FOR BURIAL IN THE ANCIENT CHRISTIAN TRADITION

J. Mark & Elizabeth J. Barna

SECOND EDITION

DIVINE ASCENT PRESS
MANTON, CALIFORNIA
MMXVII

DIVINE ASCENT PRESS
Monastery of Saint John of Shanghai and San Francisco,
PO Box 439, Manton, California 96059
www.divineascent.com

The Psalms quoted in this book are an original translation of the Greek Septuagint Psalter by Donald Sheehan. His entire Psalter was published posthumously in 2013. Used by permission of Wipf and Stock Publishers. www.wipfandstock.com

All other Scripture readings and quotations are from the Revised Standard Version of the Bible, copyright 1952, 1971, by the Division of Christian Education of the National Council of the Churches of Christ in the United States of America. Used by permission. All rights reserved.

COVER ILLUSTRATION: Mark Barna
COVER DESIGN: Chuck Bates, Charleston, South Carolina

ISBN: 978-0-9864011-0-7

The authors have given their best efforts to providing accurate, factual information regarding the matters discussed within. The authors, however, are not attorneys or health care professionals and the information within is provided for information purposes only and should not be considered legal or medical advice. Readers should seek legal counsel before taking any actions which may have legal consequences. Additionally, as the matters addressed herein may change over time and vary by locale, the authors, editors, and publishers of this work cannot and do not make any medical or legal representation regarding the accuracy of these matters as discussed herein. The reader must verify all such matters with the appropriate local legal and medical authorities and/or local legal counsel.

TO THE GLORY OF GOD.

Dedicated to Bill and Josh.
GOD GRANT THEM MANY YEARS!

In blessed memory of:
Zoran, Leigh Ann, Subdeacon Donatos,
Michael and Mary, Paul and Louise,
Ella and Frank.
MAY THEIR MEMORY
BE ETERNAL!

With grateful thanks to:
Archpriest John Breck, Priest John Parker,
Archpriest John Bethancourt, Hieromonk
Herman (Majkrzak), Julius Fielding, Michael
Breck, Xenia Sheehan, Chuck and Suzanne
Bates, and Andrew and Juliana Gould.
MAY GOD GRANT THEM ALL
MANY, MANY YEARS!

A Christian ending to our lives, painless,
blameless and peaceful; and a good
defense before the dread judgment seat
of Christ, let us ask of the Lord.
—ANCIENT CHRISTIAN PETITION

"Tell the people: though I am dead, I am still alive."
— SAINT JOHN THE
WONDERWORKER (1896–1966)
ARCHBISHOP OF SAN FRANCISCO

Come fire and cross and grapplings with wild beasts, cut-
tings and manglings, wrenching of bones, hacking of limbs,
crushings of my whole body, come cruel tortures of the devil
to assail me. None of these frighten me. One thing alone I
want and desire: only be it mine to attain unto Jesus Christ.
— SAINT IGNATIUS OF ANTIOCH (C. 50–107)
On the way to his martyrdom at Rome

Contents

Foreword

HOW SHOULD CHRISTIAN PEOPLE prepare for death, their own and that of loved ones? No question can be more important than this, since death is the final reality of our earthly life. Yet particularly in the United States, we tend to avoid the question as much as we can. We consider death to be brutal and tragic, whatever its circumstances and causes. It marks an end to our ambitions, while it underscores the ephemeral nature of our existence. Therefore we treat it like a "last enemy" from which there is no escape, no salvation. Death appears as a specter, a menacing evil, that evokes a reaction of dread. Those who conceive of it as literally a "dead end" can easily resonate with the cynical haiku:

> We live and we die.
> We make hardly a ripple.
> The question is, "Why?"

Of all people, Christians have reason to rejoice at the thought of death. The pain and anguish that surround death and the dying process are due to separation from those we love, rather than to the phenomenon itself. This, at least, is how it should be. Yet Christians as much as anyone else have gone to elaborate lengths to hide the reality of death, to mask what they mistakenly consider to be its destructive effects and its finality. This has led them, with most others, to succumb to what Jessica Mitford famously described and decried as "The American Way of Death." This is what has favored development of the lucrative funeral industry, with its unctuous directors selling over-priced burial goods to a vulnerable yet all too willing public. This is also what has led Christians to ignore the basic message of the Gospel, God's promise to His people and to all of creation, expressed so eloquently in the Orthodox Paschal hymn: "Christ is risen from the dead, trampling down death by death; and to those in the tombs He has given life!" Death has been trumped – it has been overthrown, destroyed, by the Resurrection of Jesus Christ, the eternal Son of God.

How should Christian people prepare for death? And how, once a death has occurred, in the family or church community, should they proceed, in order to assume final responsibility for the deceased by preparing the body, completing the burial, and caring for the bereaved?

Deacon Mark and Elizabeth Barna have devoted years to caring for ill and dying relatives. They have studied in depth the Church's traditional methods for facing death and caring for the departed, and they have done the requisite research in medical and legal areas, to ensure that their own ministry will offer the kind and quality of care they would want all of us to enjoy. This book represents the fruit of their quest and their experience.

Written in a genial, conversational style, this book offers the Christian reader a solid foundation in both the theology and the psychology of death: its place within God's creative and saving work, and the personal impact it makes on those facing death and those who grieve for them. It also clarifies a great many misconceptions held by most people concerning professional funeral practices, making clear that a truly "Christian ending" to our life can mean beauty and utter simplicity both in the rituals that surround it and in the burial itself. Many readers will be surprised to learn that it is not at all necessary, legally or practically, to use the services of a funeral home. There is indeed "another way," one more in keeping with the Gospel imperative to honor the physical body as a temple of the Holy Spirit.

This work includes a section on the actual preparation of the body of the deceased, together with prescribed readings of psalms and prayers, all of which can be accomplished with or without the participation of clergy. Finally, an extensive bibliography is followed by a useful list of items needed for preparation, as well as various postmortem forms the reader will find indispensable.

We owe the Barnas a great measure of thanks for the work they have done in compiling the valuable information contained in this book. One can only hope that it will guide many Christians who suffer the loss of someone close to them, in family or community, to understand better the true meaning of death as a passage from this world to eternal life in Christ. At the very least, it will provide them with practical advice and insight as to how best to confront the reality of death and the often difficult responsibility to care appropriately for the deceased.

For those who read it attentively, out of their own faith tradition, it can provide as well a new and precious perspective on the reality of death and on the most appropriate way to prepare those who have gone before us to enter into the fullness of life. Through our ministrations, as outlined here, may we commit them to the God of life and of love, the "God of the living and not of the dead," and may their memory in Him be truly eternal.

Father John Breck

Introduction

Well death don't have no mercy in this land.
He'll come to your house and he won't stay long.
Look around the room one of your family will be gone.
Death don't have no mercy in this land.

— REV. GARY DAVIS

MARK'S MOTHER DIED AT OUR HOME EARLY ONE SPRING AFTER-
NOON. This was unusual because most people who die of natural causes
die at 3 AM. She had lived with us for six years. The last five years she
was bed ridden with Alzheimer's and she couldn't speak. A broken hip
put her in bed. Mark's dad also lived with us for three of those years
with Parkinson's disease until he died of cancer. Elizabeth's dad, Frank
was also there for five years. He had Alzheimer's and a broken hip and
he was bed ridden for the last year of his life.

When Louise died we immediately called our priest and began
reading the Psalms by her bedside. Fr. John and Jeanette arrived and
took over reading while Elizabeth and I did what we had done so many
times before. We washed her hair and her entire body there in her bed.
We gave her a manicure and a pedicure. Then we took the extra step
of anointing her from head to toe with a special fragrant olive oil that
we make ourselves. We dressed her in one of her Sunday dresses. The
two men lifted her and carried her into our front room where her casket was waiting. We placed her in it and continued reading the psalms.

Hospice supplied the death certificate and we filled in the blanks.
Then Mark took it to the County Department of Vital Records. They
recorded it, made copies for him and issued a Burial, Removal and
Transport Permit. We held vigil in our home that night.

1

In the morning our sons, rented a cargo van and came to the house. We loaded their grandmother into the van and drove her to the church where we had the traditional funeral service. Then we carried her back to the van and drove, in a caravan, to Saints Mary and Martha monastery two hours away. We buried her in the monastery cemetery filling the grave ourselves.

It was a very intimate personal and loving way to care for a departed loved one. Once you've buried a loved one this way, you'll never want to turn them over to a professional again.

Since the publication of the first edition of this book, we have been amazed by the reception it has had. We thought that most people would think we were nuts. To our surprise, the vast majority of readers have been very appreciative. In the past ten years we have prepared dozens of people for burial in the manner we describe here. In our parish, when someone dies we assume the church will take care of everything. We have a good working relationship with two funeral homes and there are many ways that we can work together to serve the family, but we can also do it all ourselves, saving the family enormous amounts of money. Not only have family members approved of what we do, they have insisted on helping with the preparation. Some of them are still thanking us today for the opportunity to perform this final, simple, yet powerful service for their loved one.

With this second edition provide some insights into what we have learned over the years. One failing of the first edition was our lack of understanding of the cremation crisis among Christians. We simply assumed that Orthodox Christians understood that we do not cremate. In this edition we correct that oversight. We also include some of the techniques we have learned and dropped some practices we have eliminated. We have thoroughly updated the information given in each chapter, especially the forms in Appendix B. We hope you approve.

Death Don't Have No Mercy

Americans practice a unique form of death ritual. Our current practices are as curious as any found in folklore or those discovered by archaeologists. One can only wonder what future anthropologists might surmise from the remains they find in America a thousand years from now. As with current archeological digs, scientists will try to use these remains to understand the spirit of the times in which we live.

The spirit of our time is Consumerism. Our national economy is based on the acquisition of stuff: money, power, pleasure and all the things of this world. Early Christians would say that these distractions of everyday life are designed precisely to divert us from the remembrance of death. If only we carried the remembrance of our own death with us daily, would we be so concerned with our own acquisitions? How differently would we live if we really understood, that truly, "we can't take it with us"?

As our culture strays further and further from God, we strive with manic intensity to acquire more and more stuff to try to fill that hole that only He can fill. There will never be enough stuff to fill that hole in each of us where the infinite God should dwell. "If a man loves Me, he will keep My word, and My Father will love him, and We will come to him and make Our home with him" (John 14:23).

Pride has become a virtue and virtue a curse. Our popular culture is full of arrogance and pride in our appearance, education, erudition, wealth, power, or sexual prowess.

As Christians we are not bound to this world but to our Lord God and Savior, Jesus Christ. As believers we no longer live for ourselves; rather our life and death are in the service of the Lord. Seeing Him in our neighbor, we serve Him, love Him and care for Him in every way, at every possible opportunity. The prospect of death is still a very real, awesome and frightening mystery. Even so, seeing Him as Creator, Benefactor and Redeemer, we look forward to our heavenly birthday with anticipation and joy. "For to me to live is Christ, and to die is gain … My desire is to depart and be with Christ, for that is far better" (Philippians 1:21–23).

The Church cares for and sanctifies every facet of life, from before our birth, through baptism, marriage and the funeral. Here in America though, we have created a gap in the continuity of that care from the moment of death until the funeral. It is now our custom to turn the bodily preparation of our deceased brothers' and sisters' remains over to strangers in the funeral industry to "make the arrangements" for burial. We have been falsely persuaded by the funeral industry that most of their arrangements are required by law, and that we have very few real options, all of them expensive.

Burying the dead has always been recognized by the Church as one of our responsibilities along with visiting the sick, clothing the naked, feeding the hungry, ransoming captives and sheltering the homeless. But what does "bury the dead" mean? For most of us it has come to mean simply showing up at the funeral service.

There is a movement now among the baby boom generation, and the ecology-minded, away from the American industrialized way of dying, and back to a more traditional, communal, eco-friendly burial. Without realizing it, these groups have stumbled onto the traditional Christian form of burial. The remains of the deceased are prepared and cared for in community and returned to the earth as soon as possible, often without the assistance of a funeral home or a funeral director at all. Most states have no laws requiring embalming, caskets, vaults or crypts. While this new practice is very traditional and environmentally friendly, these groups have discovered the form without its core of meaning and substance.

Elizabeth's mother's death revealed to us the importance of our prayer for "a Christian ending to our lives." Ella died at home under hospice care. Discussing it later we decided, "That was about as good a way to die as one could ask, under the circumstances."

A Sweet Goodbye

The call came around 11:00 AM in the middle of a busy work day. Elizabeth said, "The hospice nurse just called. Today is the day. Come to Dad's house *now*."

Ella fought breast cancer for three years. We thought everything was fine until she started acting a little strange. Tests showed that the cancer had metastasized in her brain.

The next six months were very difficult as we watched Ella undergo treatment, weaken and lose weight. By the end of her course of treatment there was no reason for Ella to be in the hospital. She stayed in her own home where Frank did his best to care for her. We answered several midnight calls for help. The assistance of our local hospice was invaluable.

That last day we sat with Frank by Ella's bedside in the living room. We prayed and sang hymns and psalms. She responded enough to let us know that she knew we were there.

Later that evening Mark had to run to the church on an errand. As he returned, Elizabeth was sitting on the side of the hospital bed where she had been praying, holding her mother's hand. The house was quiet. The only light came from the kitchen. She looked up and said tearfully, "She just left."

We prayed and waited for the hospice nurse and the mortuary to come. By about 2:00 AM it was all over and we had turned Ella's remains over to strangers.

This is the American way of death. Until the beginning of the hospice movement, Ella might not even have been allowed to die at home. She probably would have died in a hospital, with machines, monitors, tubes and strangers around her. Her family may not even have seen her until the viewing at the funeral home.

Why?

Americans don't want to think about death. We ignore it and try not to think about it. We fear it. We rely on our technology and medical miracles to take every heroic measure to prolong life at all costs. When death comes we may even choose to be frozen, to await some future technological miracle. In many ways we try to act as though death were optional. When the time comes we prefer to be as far away from the dying person as possible.

It is our hope that this book may help Christians redeem our way of dying and perhaps begin to curtail, at least partially, the practice of placing the care of our deceased brothers and sisters in Christ into the hands of strangers.

Life Goes On

A few years after Ella's death, we moved to a mid-century ranch style house in a less desirable part of town, which we remodeled for handicapped access in anticipation of Frank's arrival. Frank was deteriorating mentally, as was Louise. We knew it would be difficult but we had to convince Mark's mom and dad to move in with us too. We sold Frank's house and moved him in with us in March 2004. A month later Paul and Louise arrived "for an Easter visit" and never left. Here we cared for our parents until Louise's death in April 2010. Our Lord provided us with our own family nursing home/hospice where we gave our parents our final gift to them, high quality care and a truly Christian way of dying.

Should this be where our care and service end? Like many others in the "sandwich generation," we feed, clothe, medicate, and change diapers and bedding every day and night. After their inevitable death, should we just call in the strangers to finish the job? Not at all! We are convinced that it is the duty, honor and privilege of every Christian to care for the remains of our deceased brethren.

We are not alone in our interest in caring for our own. Several churches in the United States have begun to redeem the process and start caring for their own dead to varying degrees. Some are buying land and establishing cemeteries. Most funeral directors are familiar with the preparation of Orthodox Jews for burial and can assist as needed.

Embalming, mummification and cremation were practiced by many pagan cultures for thousands of years. However, Jews believed that the body of the deceased had to be treated with the utmost respect. Mummification, chemical embalming and cremation are all violent acts that require extreme violation of the temple of the body. This could not be tolerated by Jews or Christians. The preparation of the dead was very important to the living members of the family and the community, for dealing with their grief.

The first Christians also believed that the body should be returned to the earth as quickly as possible. By this, we do not mean just the time between death and burial but also the process of bodily decay. Ideally the body would be wrapped in a shroud or baptismal garment and "planted" in contact with the earth so that it could return as quickly as possible from whence it came. "Truly, truly, I say to you, unless a grain of wheat falls into the earth and dies, it remains alone; but if it dies, it bears much fruit. He who loves his life loses it, and he who hates his life in this world will keep it for eternal life" (John 12:24–25).

Natural burial also allows our Lord to work His will as He chooses. There are incorrupt relics (bodies) all around the world, for example the incorrupt remains of Saint John Maximovich in San Francisco. God, in fact, is the only one who can truly preserve and sanctify bodily remains. "For Thou wilt not abandon my soul to Hades, nor let Thy Holy One see corruption" (Psalms 16:10; Acts 2:27).

Many funeral directors are quite willing to help provide the services required of them. Some mortuaries allow members of churches to prepare the body in their facilities. Hospices and hospitals can be quite helpful in that regard. Funeral homes are willing to help with transport, legal paperwork and other necessities, but all these things can be accomplished in community without the expense.

There are numerous options available—from the complete "home funeral," with no funeral director at all, to something short of the full-on directed funeral with embalming, $30,000 airtight casket, escort by a phalanx of black Cadillacs and placement in a sealed vault in the most "select" section of the cemetery. For this reason, we plan to focus our efforts on describing the ideal traditional ancient Christian burial, which can be accomplished completely by the family and the church at virtually no cost. This ideal may not be possible for you or your community at this time. Having the ideal in mind may help as compromises are made along the way.

In the end the traditional American way of dying is still about profit.

Like any good salesman, a successful funeral director will offer you the most expensive casket, flowers, lining, vault, crypt and other options to add to his bottom line. Often when we say "No," we feel as if we are somehow failing our loved one. There are numerous accounts of people who died while still paying for their spouse's funeral.

This book is our humble effort to help fill the gap in our care for our brethren in Christ. It is not meant to be a theological treatise about death and dying but a practical handbook for the care and preparation of bodily remains according to ancient Christian tradition.

There is little information in scripture regarding this tradition. We have some information from current and ancient sources regarding Jewish practice. Likewise, from the day of Pentecost in 33 AD, the Apostles and their disciples wrote about the daily life of the Church and how Christians should apply the Scriptures to their daily lives. Some of these writings describe the care and preparation of bodies for burial.

This great wealth of writing is available today from many sources. Some of them are listed in the bibliography at the end of this book. As Orthodox Christians, we have made extensive use of the writings of the great early luminaries of the Christian faith. These holy men came to be known as the Holy Fathers of the Christian Faith.

We would need several volumes to quote even a fraction of the scripture, patristic writings and scientific texts we have read on this subject. For those who prefer a more scholarly, heavily footnoted approach we provide a bibliography and we beg your forgiveness.

What follows is simply the result of our research, which we have gathered for our own use and that of our parish. We have been encouraged to make this information available to the Church, to encourage others to redeem the time and the process of preparation of the dead as a holy, communal activity of service and love.

Through the years we have rendered this service numerous times for friends, family and strangers. It has proven to be one of the most challenging services we can provide. Every person involved has been awed by the power of this simple act.

We are Orthodox Christians and we cannot help but approach this topic, and all of life, from this perspective. We are certain that, regardless of your own belief, there is helpful information here for everyone. We have done our best to make a difficult topic interesting and helpful for Christians, non-Christians, agnostics and atheists alike.

We begin the book by taking a brief look at the history of some of the rituals and developments that have brought us to where we are today in America. Then we look at a more scriptural and traditional Christian view of death and dying. We give detailed instructions on the preparation of the human body for a dignified, traditional Christian burial, followed by a patristic view of mourning and memorials for the dead. Then we offer a look at how we can deal with the legal maze that awaits us as we near the end, and we propose ways to address that maze in community. Finally, in our boldness, and begging your forgiveness, we offer a service of prayers and readings to be used during the process of preparation. Our aim is to try, in all humility, to help redeem that short, often forgotten snippet of time from the moment of death until the beginning of the funeral service.

Your Servants in Christ,
Mark and Elizabeth Barna

A dog is better than I am,
for he has love and does not judge.
— SAINT XANTHIAS

PART ONE

1.

An Anthropology of Burial

Therefore from one man, and him as good as dead,
were born descendants as many as the stars of heaven
and as the innumerable grains of sand by the seashore.
— HEBREWS 11:12

My trouble soon be over
soon will have an end
Though my burden may be heavy
I won't let it crush me down.
Some day I'll rest with Jesus
And wear a starry crown.
My trouble soon be over
soon will have an end.
— BLIND WILLIE JOHNSON/TRADITIONAL

THE HUMAN PASSAGE from life to death is unique in God's creation. We are the only species on earth that is aware of its own death. We think about it, plan for it, dread it, memorialize it, embrace it consciously, or understand it as passage to another realm. This can be an isolating awareness, separating us from the rest of creation as well as from one another. Death, after all, is our final and most individual act. No one can share it with us.

At the same time, our common humanity draws us together with others to form bonds of family and community. We seek each other out. We long for permanent, lifelong relationships. We are even willing to die for the sake of others. As a result we usually die in a community

13

or family group, leaving remains that the living must either deal with or ignore.

The bonds we form generally will not allow us simply to discard or ignore the death and remains of our friends, family and neighbors. As spiritual, loving beings, we feel loss. We feel the need to honor those we have known and loved. This has been true from the earliest times. Archaeologists have discovered organized, perhaps ceremonial burials dating from the Neanderthal communities of 250,000 years ago. In these graves, they have found remains carefully laid on beds of grass or reed and ringed with branches, flowers and artifacts. This is certainly a show of respect and affection. It is natural for us to honor the uniqueness of the deceased individual. It is as natural as the innate need to seek and know our Creator.

Burial as a Reflection of Life

How a man handles his own death tells us a great deal about what he believes and how he approaches his life. So it is also with cultures and societies. Through the ages of mankind upwards of 130 billion people and many cultures have come and gone, leaving evidence of numerous ways of dealing with human remains. How we treat these remains indicates much about how we live and about our attitudes toward each other, God and nature.

Inhumation is the practice of placing the body in pits, graves, urns, mounds, caves, and beneath the floors of dwellings. Sometimes bodies are embalmed or mummified. In surface burial the body is placed in hollow logs or covered with rocks or loose branches. Sepulcher burial is in a container that remains above ground, or in a special lodge, canoe, or carved stone or wooden box. Cremation burns the remains. Aerial burial places the body in tree branches, baskets, lashed to scaffolds or elevated in canoes. Aquatic burial places remains in rivers, lakes or oceans, sometimes in a boat or floating container and sometimes in a submerged box. In other cultures bodies were smoked to preserve or "cure" them.

One can surmise that each of these forms of burial developed from a particular outlook on life and a particular relationship with the earth. Together with these forms there developed rituals reflecting a particular spiritual relationship of man to man and man to the cosmos. Rituals focus the attention of the community, transforming a communal act into a sacred act.

Inhumation is the most familiar form of burial and the most prevalent throughout history. The ancient Egyptians practiced it over 5,000 years ago. Though their greatest lasting achievements—the pyramids—would be considered a sepulcher, their commoners were buried in the earth. Giant amphorae, urns used for wine and other stores, were used as coffins in Rome and in the Middle East 2000 years ago. Some early Native Americans buried their dead in great mounds of earth over 3000 years before Christ.

Native Americans of the West and the Great Plains practiced forms of aerial burial. They lashed their dead to scaffolds in holy burial grounds.

Beginning some 3000 years ago, the Bo people of the Three Gorges region in China placed solid hewn wood coffins on posts driven into the face of a cliff; the higher the coffin the more important the person. The person whose coffin fell to the ground sooner was considered the more fortunate.

Aquatic burial has been practiced in many areas where life revolved around the sea or other bodies of water. The Norse (Vikings) practiced aquatic burial, sometimes by setting ships or canoes afloat, as did several Asian cultures. Today, Navy veterans can arrange to be buried at sea from a Navy ship at no cost. It is also perfectly legal for anyone who can arrange it. Burial at sea puts the body in contact with the Earth and would be far preferable to cremation as a Christian form of burial.

Cremation has been practiced by many people, from Central and Southern Asia to Africa. It became popular in Greece around 1000 BC as a reaction to plagues. From there it spread among the aristocracy of Rome where they tried to out-do each other with huge pyres and great funeral festivals.

Elaborate funerals minimized social conflict and threats to the stability of the community. The funerals of kings, emperors and other important people served as part of an orderly transition of power. Not only did this offer lavish honor to the deceased but it also showed who was boss and previewed the new leadership.

Sepulchers were popular in the Middle East and Mediterranean areas. The word mausoleum comes from the great tomb built by Queen Artemisia for her husband, Mausolos, at Halicarnassas in the fourth century BC. Jesus Christ's holy body was buried in a sepulcher hewn from solid rock and sealed with a large stone.

As these different forms of burial developed it was necessary for the living to be involved in the handling, preparation and burial of the dead. There are many cultures in which corpse handlers were social outcasts and occupied a marginal place in the social order. This was mainly due to pagan beliefs and superstitions. Notable exceptions were the Jews and Christians. Among the Egyptians mummification was performed by priests.

It is true that in Jewish law the handling of the dead made one ritually unclean. The human body, however, bearing the image and likeness of God, was treated with great respect, and the body handlers were respected as performing a sacred duty. Today the Hevra Hadisha (burial society) in traditional Jewish communities is composed of highly regarded volunteers performing a valuable service.

Ancient Christian Burial

Christians of the early Church continued the burial traditions of the Jews. The earliest Christians, the Apostles, considered themselves Jews and spread the good news of the arrival of the Messiah and the resurrection from the dead. Therefore, death took on new meaning. Death was overcome. The human body, bearing the image and likeness of God, was not tainted but sanctified by the body and blood of Jesus Christ. A new understanding of God's great goodness and love and the goodness of creation gave a whole new insight into life and death. As gentiles received the Gospel they heard the good news of the resurrection. They abandoned their old ways of life, death and burial. Death was no longer the great terror it once was.

Ancient Christians were quite accustomed to the thought of death; it was all around them as a result of persecutions, disease, pestilence and plagues. The knowledge of one's own impending demise was ever-present. By the sixth century AD, the catacombs had become so crowded that burials began taking place outside the city. Christians continued to use church property in the cities until the eighteenth century, when these plots became hopelessly overcrowded.

> Death is a common cup all are required to drink. It is also the "divine sword" that spares no one. Death is not afraid of the king and does not honor the hierarch. It does not feel sorry for old age; it does not show mercy to beauty, nor partiality to youth. Death shows no compassion for the only child; it is not moved by tears and does not fear rulers. Death cannot be bought with money and does not take into account anyone's person nor again anyone's representative, but comes equally to all.
> — Saint John Chrysostom (c. 347–407 AD)

Through Christ we came to know the true nature of death, that it is contrary to God's will and therefore evil, the last great enemy and the great equalizer.

Each individual, king or pauper, stands before the Righteous Judge, naked and alone. The essence then of the Christian funeral is simplicity and humility. There is no great show of earthly wealth, fame or accomplishment, for all those things are dust, just as the body shall soon be. Generally a simple white shroud clothes the body to signify that all people are equal before God. Sometimes the shroud takes the form of a winding sheet, reminiscent of the swaddling clothes of a babe, to indicate the heavenly birthday of the deceased. Placed in contact with the earth, the body returns naturally to its maker and is placed in His holy hands to do with as He will.

This tradition continues today in most of the world. Jewish practice in Israel and in parts of Europe is still to bury bodies on a bed of inter-twined reeds. There is no coffin. The body is returned to the earth.

Developments Through Time

This was the typical form of burial for Christians through most of his-tory, though there have certainly been exceptions. The Black Plague of the middle ages forced the use of mass graves, and people sometimes resorted to cremation through fear of infection. Mass graves have often been used for paupers or during times of epidemics, wars and plagues.

Great plagues and epidemics struck terror into whole generations of Europeans. Many strange ideas and traditions cropped up. There was often a quite morbid curiosity about death particularly brought on by these massive losses.

With the growth of cities in Europe it became more and more com-mon to transport bodies some distance to the cemetery. This, and the fear of infection caused by the many epidemics, necessitated the use of boards and then boxes to carry the body. Coffins began to be used and later were adopted for burial in church cemeteries as well. Land for burial around churches was limited and became even more limited as cities grew larger.

In the United States and Europe cemeteries have been known for their impermanence. Many are historical sites, but many more have been turned to other uses.

Coffins take time, trouble and expense to build, and they delay the absorption of the body into the surrounding soil. In 1580, the town of Rye, Sussex, England, decreed that under no circumstances were the poor to be buried in coffins or chests, and that anyone making such a coffin should be fined ten shillings. Coffins for the poor were not only causing undue expense, but the delay in the decay of the corpse meant that the grave could not be reused as quickly. Until the eighteenth cen-tury, few people except the very rich were buried in a coffin.

In England, some graves were as much as twenty-five feet deep, with coffins stacked on top of each other to within a couple of feet of the surface. Often, because of overcrowding, after ten years or so the graves were dug up and the bones were sometimes reburied in a smaller container or transferred to a charnel house (from Latin meaning flesh) or an ossuary (bone house). Though they are unfamiliar to Americans, ossuaries are still common in Orthodox Christian monasteries and some areas of Europe. The presence of bones and skulls in everyday life serves as a constant reminder of our own mortality.

The concept of perpetual care is uniquely American. It evolved from the family farm cemetery and an abundance of cheap land. The town and church cemetery eventually turned into private, for-profit cemeteries with all the amenities. Cemeteries are also very profitable since you can get 500 graves in an acre.

Christians are aware that all that we have is a gift from God. We possess nothing that He has not bestowed upon us. We forget this sometimes and succumb to constant messages from the world telling us to "be your own master" and "take control of your own destiny." We often act as if we might live forever. As Christians, though, we realize that we are not guaranteed our next breath. Indeed, we do not have dominion over our next heartbeat. Even that is a gift from God. The Fathers of the ancient Church instruct us to be ever mindful of this fact. At any moment we may be called to account for our entire life. The ossuary is a natural and very potent reminder of that fact.

The First Undertakers

Undertakers appeared in England in the seventeenth century. Before then the laying out and preparation of the body were the responsibility of the family and were usually done by the females. Tombstones were rarities before the late seventeenth century. Gardens came to be regarded as the ideal final resting place. Flowers have been placed on corpses since prehistoric times.

Around 1700, attachments between people became a more publicly acknowledged part of life. During the Romantic Period, ideas such as the beautiful death, the cult of memory and exaggerated mourning rituals developed.

In colonial America, death was treated as a familiar part of everyday life, just as it had once been in Europe. Adults died young and the death of children was a regular occurrence. Early settlers in America buried their dead on their farms. From colonial days until the nineteenth century, the American funeral was almost exclusively a family affair. Generations of family lived in the same house or on the same farm. The family and close friends performed most of the duties in connection with the funeral. The corpse lay in the family parlor. Houses were designed with a room having doors wide enough to permit pallbearers to enter and exit carrying a coffin.

Mourners took turns watching over the body. The "wake" had a practical aspect of watching for signs of life; for the deceased to wake. Families dug graves for their own dead. Single grave sites were used to bury successive generations of the family. Later, as towns grew up, the church became the focus for burials. Bodies were generally placed in a coffin on a layer of sawdust, wood shavings or bran, sometimes a mattress.

Beginning in the 1800s, in America, some carpenters advertised themselves as coffin makers. Church sextons not only rang the steeple bells, but also dug graves. Stable keepers provided carriages. Ornate hearses became popular in the late 1800s and came complete with glass windows, coach lamps, carved pillars and heavy, tasseled draperies. Matched teams of beautiful, well-trained horses drew the funeral coach. The United States passed laws forbidding the interruption of burial or the seizure of a body as collateral for a debt.

By this time, American attitudes, especially those of the white middle class, were similar to those of Europeans. Victorians were obsessed with death. Infant mortality was high and many died before old age as a result of disease, injury or infection. Cities grew, bringing people into closer and closer proximity to each other. Sewers and sanitation were still primitive at best, as were hospitals. Doctors had none of the knowledge of microbes and pharmaceuticals that we take for granted today. Industries expanded in the cities with little care for their employees' health or safety.

Premature burials and the fear of them were a terrifying fact of life. The recycling of graves led to the discovery of evidence that people had been buried alive, causing widespread fear. Numerous inventions were designed to detect life or to save the person who was buried prematurely. Some people went to extremes, leaving instructions that they be decapitated or to otherwise insure they were dead before being buried.

Over time, some small church graveyards were not well maintained and, as towns grew, civic authorities took them over. In 1763, all church cemeteries in Paris were closed and municipal cemeteries were opened outside the city. Municipal cemeteries were unknown in England until the 1820s. In 1806 the New York board of health recommended that city burial places be converted into public parks. Laws to that effect were passed and finally enforced in 1822.

2.

The Development of an Industry

Gracious dying is a huge, macabre and expensive joke on
the American public. — JESSICA MITFORD

Cultural Factors

WITH THE INDUSTRIAL REVOLUTION came many cultural and demographic shifts. People left their farms and moved to the cities, all but destroying the extended rural family. Urban culture became one of man against nature in an effort to control one's environment and circumstances.

The family also changed as its members became detached and separated. More and more, people ended up in hospitals to receive care for illness or injury or, as time went on, for childbirth, rather than at home. Death moved to the hospital as well, away from public view.

As the family changed, so did the architecture of the home. Funerals had once taken place in the home parlor. Now that embalming began to remove the corpse from the house, undertakers offered their own parlors for the "laying out" of the dead, and care for the dead was taken out of the hands of their loved ones. This precipitated a loss of intimacy with the reality of death.

The causes of death changed as well. In the past, many people tended to die quickly, killed by accident or disease or childbirth. Then industrial diseases and accidents became major factors along with sanitation problems in the big cities. Today, with cancer and heart disease the leading causes of death, diseases last longer, becoming more frightening. Our fear of disease makes death itself repellent, at least in part because it's been so hidden from us. In-hospital death is now an exercise in technology. People die the death of their disease or the one assigned by medical technology.

Advances in medicine have led to death as a moment in time being replaced by death as a process. Our technology makes the time of death, in some cases, remarkably difficult to define. In the United States, the only point at which death is recognized is when the brainstem itself has stopped functioning. The declaration of death in hospital occurs only when the last trace of brain function is gone. This determination can be made only with the aid of sophisticated high-tech equipment. In effect, patients require permission to die, and they are expected to follow hospital rules in doing so.

Hospitalization of death banished the emotions. Mourning faded away in a community disconnected from the death of its own members. Any sense of solidarity among the members of the community was replaced by a mass of dispersed individuals competing their way to the top. In a society based on competitiveness, winning and the accumulation of "stuff," the wasting death of disease and even old age is the final shame of ultimate defeat.

As people were further and further removed from handling death, a mystique grew up around it. It became something we had no familiarity with, knew little about, were afraid to touch or even think about. We lost our capacity to face its darkness. Instead we attempt simply to banish it from our consciousness. We can ignore the scandal of death (which cannot be prevented) and force the bereaved into silence, or we can pretend indifference and call death merely a natural event, either a dissolution into nothingness or a natural transition into some larger cosmos. The result, for individuals and communities, is that we have lost the emotional, sociological and spiritual resources we need to face death directly.

How did this modern denial of death come to supplant the bittersweet joy of the last communion between the dying and survivors?

Only in the light of Christ do we see any hope to take us through the hopelessness of death. Christianity offers the only sensible explanation for questions asked by all mankind such as, "Why am I here?" and "Why must I die?" As we will see in chapter 5, it is only in the light of Jesus Christ that we learn the answer to both questions is, "Because we are loved."

Modern Death

To embalm means to cover or impregnate with fragrant ointments called "balms." Various forms of embalming were used by several pagan cultures as well as ancient Christians. About five thousand years ago, Egyptians began to use embalming and mummification for religious purposes.

Christians refused mummification because it was a pagan practice that violated the corpse. Understanding the body to be a gift from God and the temple of the Holy Spirit, neither Christians nor Jews could allow it to be desecrated by removal of the organs and fluids in a vain attempt to preserve it. The type of embalming we use today was mostly abandoned for nearly 1500 years. The nineteenth-century, Industrial-Revolution ethos of man against nature revived interest in it.

In traditionally Orthodox Christian countries of Eastern Europe, Russia and the Middle East, chemical embalming and American-style industrial funerals are mostly unheard of. These cultures maintain the Christian traditions of close family and community involvement. This is true also in most other European countries and around the world. The type of funeral most Americans are used to is virtually unique to America.

Modern chemical embalming originated during the Civil War. Dr. Thomas Holmes experimented with preservative chemicals as a coroner's assistant in New York. He received a commission in the Army Medical Corps and was assigned to Washington, DC, where he began to use chemicals to embalm officers killed in battle. When he realized the commercial potential of his method, he resigned his commission and began offering his service to the public for $100. In 1867, with the discovery of formaldehyde, embalming entered the modern age.

Every occupation wants to be respected. The greater the need for the profession, the more respect for it and the higher the income. Modern chemical embalming is the magic potion that transformed undertakers from tradesmen practicing the "dismal trade" of the nineteenth century into twentieth-century professionals. Here was something only the undertaker could do. In addition, he learned the tricks to add a lifelike appearance to a corpse and present it beautifully to the family and the public. Sometimes corpses were displayed in shop windows, the undertaker being justifiably proud of his handiwork. Chemical embalming and the art of presentation gave "the profession" the respectability it had long desired.

Embalming gave twentieth-century funeral directors the authority to promote their service in a credible, scientific and profitable way. Embalming is the very heart and soul of the industry. One mortician's textbook, quoted in Jessica Mitford's *The American Way of Death Revisited*, calls embalming "the very foundation of modern mortuary service—the factor which has made the elaborate funeral home and lucrative funeral service possible." Ironically, the invention of refrigeration around the turn of the twentieth century made embalming obsolete.

Industrialization, consumerism, faith in science and technology, and humanism undercut the relevance of religion in everyday life. The rhythm of life is greatly changed and death is no longer part of the rhythm. It is now something we leave to specialists.

Today, western society feeds on a steady diet of death in books, movies and television as entertainment. Yet real death, that of friends, family and coworkers, is hidden away and denied as much as possible by the industrial funeral complex which we have created.

The hospice movement defies the conventional denial of death. Staffed by nurses, psychologists and social workers, the hospice can also relieve loved ones who cannot provide the high level of care required but who wish to honor the patient's need for human warmth. Hospice caregivers help remove death from the institution. Through death education, they encourage openness and frank discussion about life and death options and offer support for both the living and the dying.

Modern Burial

Death in modern society is almost shameful and taboo. For most people today, death is virtually invisible. Consequently, the bereaved and the dying alike can find themselves isolated. Ushering the body from death bed to grave has fallen to specialists, referred to first as undertakers, then morticians, and now, funeral directors. This evolution of terms is indicative of our times, in which the "traditional" American funeral is more of a pageant and display rather than a sacred ritual. The modern funeral is focused on creating a beautiful memory picture worthy of a true Hollywood director.

Archaeologists "might rashly conclude that twentieth-century Am-erica was a nation of abjectly imitative conformists, devoted to machine-made gadgetry and mass-produced art of a debased quality; that its dominant theology was a weird mixture of primitive superstitions and superficial attitudes towards death, overlaid with a distinct tendency towards necrophilism," said Jessica Mitford, in *The American Way of Death Revisited*. There is little to argue with in that statement. As a society we are terribly afraid of the reality of our own death and do everything we can to distract ourselves from it.

So it is with our funeral, the new American tradition. The deceased is no longer a brother or sister in Christ, to be treated as God's very image and likeness. He or she becomes an *IT*; a thing to be suctioned, plugged, stapled, painted and put on display, creating a pleasing "memory picture" for the bereaved and tremendous profit for the embalmers. Their justifications fly in the face of reality, yet somehow they have managed to make their cult of death palatable and even desirable to the general public. The modern American tradition of death is itself a calculated denial of death. The deceased is made to look as though he were sleeping, not dead.

Funeral homes are mostly small operations performing fifty to a hundred funerals per year. Such slow activity in the dismal trade makes it difficult to maintain a full-time "professional" operation. How can one survive and maintain all the accouterments of elegance and success we have come to expect from our funeral homes if they produce income only one-sixth or one-third of the year? Like every other successful salesman, the funeral director must believe in himself and in his product. Hence the high cost of dying.

When marketing a funeral, the "traditional package" will be the most profitable. Trade advertisements promote "Gracious Dying" in a solid copper or eighteen-gauge, lead-coated steel casket with an adjustable inner spring mattress for maximum durability, beauty and craftsmanship. Others offer handmade original fashions for the well-dressed corpse and the ultimate in embalming cosmetics. They offer the finest care with dignity, refinement, professional service and sincerity.

The typical attitude within the profession is that in keeping with our high standard of living, we should maintain an equally high standard of dying, not to mention an equally high profit margin. The myth of "gracious living" is now the myth of "gracious dying." In 1961 one could expect to pay $750 for the typical casket and services. Today the range in our area is from $4,510 to $34,005 including casket, plus $3,000–$4,000 for a cemetery plot and basic marker.

Big Business

Today, the funeral profession has become a large industry, with numerous allied trades, consolidation and several companies listed on the New York Stock Exchange. It does not appear to be ruled at all by the laws of supply and demand. In accounting language from annual reports, "the lack of price sensitivity on the part of the consumer makes it an attractive industry." Forty-five percent of customers pick a funeral home that served someone else in the family. Thirty-three percent call the nearest mortuary (perhaps the only one in town), and eleven percent pick a funeral home based on a perceived ethnic or religious affiliation.

Funeral service has always been a for-profit business and many funeral directors try to provide fair service at a fair price. Funeral directors claim that about 120 hours go into a funeral, plus their expenses.

Our traditional ancient Christian preparation takes about forty-five minutes and can cost the family nothing.

In reaction to abuses and public complaints, the Federal Trade Commission established a General Rule regarding funeral service and pricing. Funeral homes are now required to provide a written General Price List of their services to the consumer on request. Numerous items are required to be listed but the list is not necessarily all-inclusive. If you are planning to use a funeral director for a funeral, the best advice is to be well informed and shop beforehand. The FTC publishes a guide to funerals, available on the internet or by mail.

The General Rule allows the General Price List to contain a non-declinable Basic Charge of Service fee; also known as "Professional Services." This is the absolute minimum you will pay for the services of a funeral director. Everything else is additional. No matter how little of the services you use you will still be paying for the fancy establishment and its upkeep, the embalming facilities and staff, including secretaries and parking lots you are not using. A professional services fee that used to be $400 is now $1,000 to $4,000.

The industry began to consolidate in the 1980s. Three major corporations, Service Corporation International, Loewen Group and Stewart Company are buying up funeral homes, cemeteries, crematories, casket and vault manufacturers, monument companies and florists all over North America and Europe. Their aim is "full service" control of all facets of the "post-death" process. As a result, funeral costs are eight to ten times what they were thirty years ago. Service Corporation International reported a 2016 revenue of over $3.031 billion. When the big three buy an operation they keep the old family name and usually keep the old family management under contract for a few years. You must ask specifically whether the funeral home is independent or owned by one of the large corporations.

Corporate philosophy and the vagaries of the stock markets dictate that companies either "grow or die." The Big Three are seeking to expand their markets outside the United States by selling our brand of funeral to the rest of the world. They are making inroads in the industrialized countries of Europe by capitalizing on the ecomomic boom of the late twentieth century and the secularization of those countries.

The Big Three consolidate operations such as casket supply, embalming and floral preparation into a central location, and then deliver the "product" to the individual funeral homes. Generally, in industry, such consolidation and the economies of scale bring prices down. Not so in the funeral business. SCI has ten percent of all funeral homes in prime metropolitan areas. Their prices average sixty percent higher than independent funeral homes. Their funeral homes reap a thirty-four percent profit margin and their cemeteries, twenty percent.

The type of funeral sold is limited somewhat by the customer's ability to pay; though not as much as in other industries. The number of funerals is limited by demographics, i.e. the death rate. The only way to overcome these limitations and increase profit is skillful salesmanship. If you decide to use a funeral home for a "traditional American" funeral, be careful what you wear, the kind of car you drive and, for goodness' sake, leave your Rolex at home! Funeral salesmen are very adept at sizing up customers before they even get in the door.

Like any good salesman, they study sales techniques and psychology to steer you to their most profitable items. The casket is around forty percent of the profit in a funeral. The mid-priced casket usually has the highest markup. The inexpensive cloth-covered pine casket (perfect for an ancient Christian burial) is usually so ugly no one would want to "show it off" at the viewing. Only the customers with the barest means would want this casket, which is usually hidden in the basement or warehouse. You may have to ask to see it. On the other hand, the salesperson will be proud to show you the available laser engraving of your loved one's Service logo, favorite hobby or sports franchise. If he doesn't have the cheaper model on site, it might take weeks to have one delivered, but the $20,000 cherry casket can be delivered, custom laser engraved overnight.

Cemeteries will sell you "view lots," "garden locations" or a "memorial estate." In your estate, you may be required to purchase either a grave liner or a vault. Neither is required by law, but most commercial cemeteries require one or the other to prevent the ground from settling and to increase profit. The vault is a complete concrete or fiberglass enclosure. The liner is cheaper and far better for an ancient Christian burial because it is only five-sided, with the floor open to the earth. It is then filled with earth and topped by a concrete lid. "Perpetual care" adds twenty to twenty-five percent to the cost of the plot.

There are no federal laws requiring the services of a funeral director, embalming, caskets or coffins, vaults or liners. At this writing there are no state laws requiring embalming for any reason in any state. Only ten of fifty states require any involvement of a professional funeral director. Everything needed for a proper Christian burial can be provided by the family and the church community.

If you find that you need a funeral director and a commercial cemetery, do your homework and shop around. It won't take long and this is just the type of service that a church guild or fellowship can provide. Remember, the funeral director is paid to serve you and your family. If he wants your business he must abide by your wishes and your religious sentiments. If he can accommodate Jewish customs he can certainly accommodate those of Christians wishing to maintain the ancient traditions. If he tells you, "It's the law," ask him to show you that law. If he balks, simply get up and walk out.

Know your state laws and regulations. Most, if not all, states have their entire legal code on the internet for all to see. It's not hard to find and not very difficult to read. The Statute usually just sets up a regulatory board to make regulations. The Regulations are where you will find the specifics. Remember that most state regulations are in place to regulate the professionals. You'll find in most states there are precious few regulations on church and family burials.

If you have a question about funeral law the worst place to go is to a funeral director. While assisting parishioners we have been confronted by many myths and fallacies perpetuated by funeral directors, and some lies. They have told us "the law says" we must use a licensed funeral director, we must embalm, if we don't embalm we must bury within twenty-four hours, if we don't embalm we can't have an open casket. They have also told us that we must use a licensed funeral director to transport a body across state lines for burial and we can't ship a body on an airline without a professional funeral director. These statements are all untrue. They have even asked for copies of insurance policies and bank account information to find out how much money is available. We refuse. We find it amazing that some families are willing to surrender this personal information to a business just for the asking. We operate strictly on a cash and carry basis. When we stand our ground and prove our knowledge of the law they back down. These days we have a good relationship with our local professionals. When we call they provide the services we require with a smile.

You only get one funeral. There is no second chance. Some see this as an opportunity to show off all their earthly accomplishments. We know of one bronze mausoleum plaque with the image of a golf flag and the inscription "Five Holes in One." Some may want the finest casket, the most expensive flowers and funeral cortège for the great send-off. But the limos will go home, the flowers will be thrown on the trash heap and the casket will be buried under the ground. What's it really all about?

"Vanity of vanities, says the Preacher; all is vanity" (Ecclesiastes 12:8).

In contrast, the great French President and General, Charles de Gaulle, was buried in 1970 in a plain wooden coffin made by the local carpenter. He was buried in a small village cemetery, with only his family, friends and neighbors in attendance.

3.

Funeral Madness
Annihilation of the Person

Christ is risen from the dead,
Trampling down death by death
And upon those in the tombs bestowing life.
— TROPARION OF PASCHA

Just remember death is not the end.
— BOB DYLAN

TODAY THERE ARE TWO MAIN CHOICES for the disposal of human remains, burial and cremation. The odds are that you, or someone you know, is thinking about cremation when you die. We didn't realize the extent of this problem when we wrote the first edition of *A Christian Ending*. We simply took for granted that Orthodox Christians don't cremate. To be a Christian is to believe in the physical resurrection of the body. Belief in Christ's bodily resurrection is the linchpin of Christianity (1 Corinthians 15:16—18). We greatly underestimated the level of confusion around this topic.

Our error became evident in our first call-in interview on Ancient Faith Radio. Nearly all the questions we received were about cremation. Our first few workshops showed the same level of concern and confusion. This prompted us to create our podcast series for Ancient Faith Radio.com. The topic of the first podcast we recorded was cremation. Our lack of understanding was a flaw which we now attempt to correct.

Cremation

Cremation has been marketed as "enlightened" ever since funeral directors learned how profitable it can be. Additional services are added to this low-cost option to increase profit. A top-flight funeral salesman will sell embalming and an expensive metal or cherry casket along with a viewing, a "traditional" funeral service, cremation, urn, and crypt or niche for the urn. He might even add a "perpetual care" charge to it. Cremation now accounts for well over a third of the market in the United States. Cremation rates in England approach ninety percent and in Washington State they are around eighty percent.

That means that a lot of Christians have bought into the illusion of "enlightened" cremation. Whatever the reasoning, most people still choose cremation because it is cheaper and perceived as being less emotional for the family. The Christian life, death and funeral have always reflected our Lord Jesus Christ's own extreme humility. A truly traditional ancient Christian burial can cost the family nothing and the benefits to the family and community are enormous.

Cremation has never been a valid option for Christians. It is a purely pagan practice that early Christians rejected as abominable. It undermines the biblical doctrine of the resurrection and fosters disbelief in it. The extent of its adoption by the secular world and its misunderstanding among Christians has made this a critical issue for all believing Christians, especially clergy and theologians. The magnitude of the problem makes it an issue that can no longer be ignored.

Jesus Was Buried

In any meditation about Christian burial practice we can start with our Lord's burial as our guide. Our Lord Jesus Christ was lovingly buried in a new tomb donated by a wealthy Jew. Joseph of Arimathea was honored to offer his own final resting place for Christ's tomb at the risk of his social standing and even his life. The Holy Myrrh Bearers came early, bearing spices and ointments with which to anoint Christ's precious relics.

Burial is the tradition of God's people from the very beginning of time. Cremation is a relatively new development in human history. Some anthropologists believe that the practice of burning people didn't even occur until 2500 to 2000 years before Christ. Some think that it stems from early pagan superstition and fear of the dead. Their fears were allayed by destruction of the remains.

Even before Christ's birth, inhumation of dead bodies was one of the things that separated all believers from the pagan world that surrounded them. God frequently warned the Hebrews not to adopt the values and practices of the pagans. Abraham dealt at length with Ephron the Hittite to purchase a burial place for himself and his people (Genesis 23:4—20). Then, at the end of his life he made his son Joseph swear to return him from Egypt to be buried in the place which he had bought. Joseph did so with Pharaoh's permission, since the Egyptians also practiced burial. Burial was such an important practice that all of Abraham's household made the journey as well (Genesis 47:29—50:14).

This respect for a person's remains is not just some cultural accident. God Himself buried Moses within sight of the Promised Land "and no one knows to this day where his burial place is." And the Israelites mourned him in the plains of Moab for thirty days (Deuteronomy 34:5—6).

Burial was not reserved only for the most revered in Israel but even for criminals (Deuteronomy 21:23). The Hebrews buried strangers (Tobit 1:17—18), most criminals and the indigent. Only criminals who had committed the most heinous crimes were cremated because cremation was the complete destruction of the person (Joshua 7:15). It was said that even one who was blessed by God with many possessions and a large family, if he were denied burial would be better off if he were never born (Ecclesiastes 6:3).

In the Bible, fire is mostly a symbol of evil and destruction, and a portrait of hell. In the Old Testament it was not the people who were faithful to God who were burned but those who provoked His wrath. There is not a single instance in the Old Testament when cremation had

God's blessing (Amos 2:1–2). It was a totally pagan custom not to be imitated by God's people.

To commit a body to fire is the deliberate burning of something sacred. In the Old Testament to be left unburied was to be treated as refuse (Jeremiah 25:33) and the Talmud states that "Every death which is accompanied by burning is looked upon as idolatry" (*Avoduh Zarah* 1:3).

Most of the pagan people surrounding the Jews, particularly the Romans, practiced cremation. The Hebrew tradition of burial was so well known that the first-century Roman historian Tacitus recorded that the Hebrews "bury rather than burn dead bodies." Joseph of Arimathea knew that Jesus's body would be burned, both because it was routine for the Romans and because the Jewish authorities feared him so much that they wanted Him destroyed. Joseph buried Him because of Jewish law (Deuteronomy 21:23), to fulfill the Old Testament prophecies (Psalm 34:20), and to affirm Jesus's own words (Matthew 26:12).

Jesus attacked many Jewish traditions but burial was not one of them. His dear friend Lazarus was buried. Christ raised him from the dead to show the reality of bodily resurrection and to prepare His disciples for His own resurrection, not because he was buried in the ground.

The earliest Christians opposed all abominable pagan practices such as infanticide, child abandonment, abortion, human sacrifice and suicide because of the sanctity of the human person, of whom the body is the most visible, present and sensible part. The human being is the most sacred and valuable element of all creation. We are not something to be trivialized with wild parties, brutalized with violent embalming or destroyed by cremation. Nor are we to be idolized by ancestor worship, but respectfully placed back into the loving hands of the One who made us.

Early Christians didn't separate the dead into a separate category. Being baptized into Christ and having overcome death there was no longer any reason to do so since, within the body of Christ, there is no longer any separation.

The Roman emperor Julian the Apostate (d. 363) said that the care that Christians showed to those who had died was one of the reasons for Christianity's widespread growth. They rushed to recover the bodies of martyrs, often at the risk of their own lives. They lovingly washed and buried even the victims of plagues (St. John Chrysostom, Homily 84). Even during wars they considered it their duty to bury their pagan enemies as well as their Christian brethren.

Burial is also one of the practices that made Christians so hated by the Romans. The Roman critic Caecilius wrote angrily, "They curse our funeral pyres and condemn cremation." (Octavius 11) Christians abhorred cremation not just because it represents a materialistic understanding of the universe and a denial of the resurrection. To the early Christians, to cremate was to deny the resurrection, and to deny the resurrection was to deny Christ Himself.

Christians who were willing to be beheaded, devoured by wild beasts, boiled in oil or hung on a cross rather than burn a piece of incense in a pagan temple would never have accepted burning the body of Christ, of which we are all members. To commit a body to destruction by fire is the deliberate burning of something sacred. Every person noted to have died in the New Testament was buried.

Early Church canons didn't address the issue of cremation simply because it wasn't an issue. No prohibition was needed because Christians abhorred the practice. The early Church Father Tertullian attacked the severity of cremation saying, "What pity is that which mocks its victims with cruelty." (*On the Resurrection of the Flesh 1*) He called the flames of cremation "a symbol of the fire of hell." The resurrection of the body assumes burial and graves. Cremation is total destruction in which the only hope is in a disembodied immortal soul.

Early Gnostic heretics denied the resurrection of the body. They believed man had only an immortal soul and that the body was unimportant. This belief continues today in Buddhism, Hinduism and other pagan sects. Hindus believe that fire purifies the soul. From the sixth-century Hindus cremated the living wife of the deceased in a practice called Suttee. This practice was outlawed by the British in 1829. Christians have never believed in violence toward the living or the dead. We know that personhood doesn't reside in either the body or the soul. It is the unique union of the two.

As Christianity gained influence in the Roman Empire, cremation slowly receded as an acceptable practice. By the later part of the fourth century, cremation rates had dropped dramatically. Charlemagne the Great (745—814) finally outlawed cremation in the Holy Roman Empire.

Cremation was virtually unknown in the western world for over a thousand years until the mid-nineteenth century. Only the bodies of the worst criminals were burned and scattered to indicate the severity of their crimes. The practice was revived among the public by atheists and freethinkers. It was attractive to spiritualists, Theosophists, Unitarians and Universalists of the time. Early cremations were pagan or atheistic services with readings from Hindu scripture and Charles Darwin. England passed the Cremation Act, making it legal in 1902. Even so, it was still quite rare into the 1930s and 1940s.

The dramatic rise in cremation rates coincides with, and appears to be related to the 1960s' counterculture, with its rejection of Christian values and the rapid secularization of society. The growth of cremation among Christians can be attributed to the decline in Biblical knowledge and standards. At the root of cremation is the denial of eternal life and the resurrection of the dead. Current practice has carried the annihilation of the person to a new level. The ancient pagans at least buried the bones as do Hindus and Buddhists of today. We crush them and scatter them to the wind.

Ironically, a generation that claimed to be about peace has chosen the most violent method to dispose of their loved one's bodily remains. Pacemakers and any other battery-powered devices must be removed before incineration or they'll explode. The body is placed a cardboard box and put into the furnace. The burners are lit and the temperature is raised to between 1,400 and 2,100 degrees F. This is maintained for approximately one hour per one hundred pounds of body weight. The burners are pointed directly on the body, not just heating it but burning it like a blowtorch. This speeds the process, and time is money.

The burning process can take up to four hours. That requires a considerable amount of fuel. It's not as environmentally friendly as people would like to believe. So, what you are left with after hours of hellish temperatures is some ash and about four pounds of dehydrated, collapsed skeleton.

Most people don't realize that bones don't burn. For the crematory to hand you an urn of ash, they must scrape the bones and ash out of the hot oven, remove any metal, and place the bones into a supersized high-speed blender that crushes the bones into fine sandy granules. Ashes are often intermixed in the crematory, and sometimes given to the wrong family. Families have found pieces of dentures and other items that couldn't have belonged to their loved one. Crematories will sometimes supplement the deceased's ashes with fireplace ashes or white sand to give them a more pleasing appearance.

Some people choose cremation out of a mistaken concern for the environment. Studies have shown that, besides the use of fossil fuels, the process releases high levels of dioxins and trace minerals, particulate matter, carbon monoxide, nitrogen oxides, sulfur dioxide, hydrogen chloride, and metals such as mercury, cadmium, lead dioxins and furans into the atmosphere. Some of these pollutants increase when oven temperatures are raised but they are within EPA limits.

Crematories are unregulated in half the states in the United States. Lack of regulation leads to abuses. Headlines over the years have told of some of the more egregious practices such as burying corpses in mass graves to avoid the cost of fuel. Bodies have also been sold to mortuary science schools and medical schools.

Still the main reason people choose cremation is perceived cost savings. It is true that cremation can be cheaper than a professionally directed funeral with limousines, hearse and flower car. It is also true that a good salesman can still make cremation more profitable for the funeral home. Yet, even the cheapest basic cremation can't compare with the cost of a fully Church-directed burial without the services of a professional funeral director.

Memory Eternal

Sadly, cremation often leaves nothing for loved ones to remember or gather around. Families used to gather at the cemetery, particularly during the Paschal season, to remember loved ones, pay their respects and sing "Christ is Risen." When ashes are scattered, where do we go? What do we do? Studies have shown that we forget. Over five percent of people never pick up the ashes at the crematory and they rarely erect monuments or memorials. The fact is that, all too often, cremated people are simply forgotten. This seems to validate the traditional Christian abhorrence of complete annihilation.

For the Christian who believes that "we are surrounded by so great a cloud of witnesses," this is not acceptable. We pray that God will hold our loved ones eternally in His memory. For when God remembers us we exist. If God ceases to remember us we cease to exist. We sing "memory eternal" at the funeral and at memorial services to show our trust in the mercy of God that He will hold our loved one eternally in His memory.

As Christians we've tried to place ourselves completely in His hands, surrendering ourselves to His Holy Will. In the end we place our body into His hands, in the earth from which He made us. Maybe He'll preserve our bodies and future generations will have our relics to venerate, maybe not. Regardless, it is His choice not ours.

Relics

The term "relics" refers, in general, to the remains of any Christian. More specifically, though, the term refers to the "incorrupt" relics of Saints. All over the world there are relics of Saints of the Church which have never decomposed. These relics often are wonderworking relics responsible for many healings. Some are even known as "myrrh gushers" because the relics stream with the fragrant oil emanating from within. The oil is collected and used to anoint the sick, often with miraculous results.

If you would like to visit the incorrupt relics of a great wonderworking Saint you need to travel no further than to San Francisco, California. At the Orthodox Cathedral of Our Lady Joy of All Who Sorrow on Geary Street, you can reverence the relics of Saint John Maximovich the Wonderworker of Shanghai and San Francisco. Saint John died in 1966. His un-embalmed body was placed in a coffin and taken to a room in the basement of the cathedral. Over time the room was improved and painted with iconography, becoming a chapel. Numerous miracles and healings took place there. In 1994, with many prayers and great solemnity, the casket was opened in preparation for St. John's beatification as a Saint of the Church. When the casket was opened, rather than the odor of decay one would expect after twenty-eight years in a basement, the attendees were enveloped by the fragrant smell of myrrh. Though the vestments were deteriorated, his body was found to be intact. His relics now rest in a reliquary in the nave of the cathedral upstairs.

More recently Mark was requested to return to Dallas, Texas as a member of the team to exhume and rebury the body of Archbishop Dmitri of Dallas, Orthodox Church in America. He was requested in Dallas five years earlier to prepare the Archbishop for burial. At that time Mark was very concerned because the cemetery required that he be buried in a vault. After five years buried in the ground the Archbishop's body was completely intact. The only damage to his body was caused by the vault, not by decomposition. The professional funeral directors on site were amazed. They said, "there should have been nothing but bones covered with goo." There wasn't even any mold inside the coffin or the vault. The Archbishop now rests in a chapel in Saint Seraphim Cathedral in Dallas.

Cremation as practiced today is total destruction of the body. There is no opportunity for relics to be collected and reverenced by the Church.

Cremation is also a prideful choice. In the end we decide what happens to our body, not God. If we choose cremation it's our choice not His; and we're choosing it in direct opposition to the teaching of His

Holy Church. After a lifetime of prayer, fasting, humility and service, why make our last act on earth an act of pride?

Chemical Embalming

On the other end of the spectrum is chemical embalming. Where cremation treats the body like waste, embalming turns it into an idol. This too is a very pagan concept. The ancient Egyptians embalmed in an attempt to preserve the body for use in the afterlife. We know better. We know that our resurrected bodies will be the same but perfected.

Modern chemical embalming is not only a form of pagan idol worship, it is simply a lie. It can only preserve a body at room temperature for three to four days. The processes of cell decomposition and putrefaction occur from the inside out. The chemicals used can only delay the process. Neither they nor the best stainless steel casket laid in a concrete vault can prevent the decay of the human body. Only God can do that.

Embalmers give three main justifications for their trade: disinfection, preservation and restoration to a semblance of lifelike appearance. Early on, it was also one of the means of preventing premature burial, making measures such as decapitation to prevent live burial no longer necessary.

Invented during the War Between the States as a means to return officers from the field to their homes for burial, chemical embalming has, in this short 150 years or so, become the Traditional American form of funeral preparation. Yet, chemical embalming was made obsolete by refrigeration a century ago.

The human body will keep perfectly well for twenty-four hours; longer with refrigeration. The industry understands this and still continues to convince the unwitting that embalming is necessary. An article in National Funeral Service Journal stated that "Sanitation is probably the furthest thing from our mind ... motives for embalming are economic and sentimental." Clearly, embalming was already entrenched in the growing funeral industry and even became the justification for the industry's existence. It is what makes the funeral industry necessary as it is the only part of the funeral process that the average person cannot do. Embalming requires a license. Anyone can refrigerate.

Modern embalming is perhaps even more violent than cremation. The eyes and mouth are sewn shut or closed with materials similar to barbed wire. Tubes are inserted into main blood vessels so the blood can be pumped out of the body and flushed down the drain while red colored embalming liquid is pumped in. A long metal tube called a trocar is inserted near the navel and used to puncture all the organs to release their blood so that it, and the organs, can be sucked out and washed into the sewer. Bodily orifices are plugged with plastic screw-like devices. Then the cosmetics are applied, the whole package is dressed and placed into an overpriced box and put on display. The entire process is very disrespectful to a child of God.

The idea of using embalming fluid as a disinfectant is simply naive. Embalming fluids are preservatives. They tend to encapsulate bacteria and viruses rather than destroy them. A United States Centers for Disease Control (CDC) report states that embalming creates a health hazard to embalmers and that "universal precautions" are now recommended. The CDC recommends gloves, face mask and body suit for all chemical embalming. In opposition to this and to new Occupational Safety and Health Administration (OSHA) standards for the protection of embalmers, the industry argued that no case of infection by dumping human bodily wastes, including blood and tissue, into sewers has ever been documented.

Nevertheless, OSHA lists about 260 chemicals that embalmers need to be protected against. And since those chemicals eventually end up in the ground and in the shallow water table, embalming is not an ecologically sound practice, despite claims of the industry to the contrary. In fact, burial vaults were originally invented to contain embalming chemicals, not body fluids.

Several Canadian provinces, along with Hawaii and Ohio, specifically forbid the embalming of bodies that have died from about a dozen infectious diseases. A British report from 1995, for example, states that opening cadavers with tuberculosis is dangerous.

Dr. Jesse Carr, former chief of Pathology of San Francisco General Hospital and Professor at the University of California Medical School, is quoted in Jessica Mitford's The American Way of Death Revisited as stating that there is no good reason for embalming. A good undertaker would do his cosmetology and then freeze the corpse.

As we have said, embalming doesn't even preserve the body in any real, long-term sense. It will only keep a body "presentable" for four to six days, depending on how well the job is done. Embalmers usually concentrate on the upper body because that is what will be seen at the viewing. The abdomen receives enough attention to prevent unwanted odors. Lower extremities receive little attention.

The only true justification for embalming is cosmetic. Embalmers put great effort into making the corpse very lifelike for viewing. The embalmer's art is a cosmetic tour de force, employing everything from super glue and barbed wire to an air brush and lighting set "just so."

That beautiful top-of-the-line, silk-lined bronze casket set under the blue lights, seals in (not out) the anaerobic bacteria in and on the corpse—the kind that grow without oxygen. Aerobic bacteria do a much better job of decomposition, but they require oxygen. One can easily understand the process of putrefaction by placing a plate of food in the refrigerator, uncovered. It dries out. Place the same plate of food in a sealed jar at room temperature and it will rot and turn into a putrefied mass. Expensive, hermetically sealed caskets have even been known to explode due to the buildup of gasses. The human body, embalmed or not, is much better off in no coffin at all.

The average funeral in America today will cost around $5,000–$10,000. Frank paid $10,000 for his casket alone. He made his own funeral arrangements just as he was slipping toward dementia, and the funeral director took full advantage of his condition.

More to Come

If embalming and cremation weren't enough, there's a host of funeral craziness out there and more coming. You can have your coffin emblazoned with the logo of your favorite sports team. Some "enlightened" folks are advocating having your body dissolved by heated alkaline chemicals and then just flushed into the sewer in a process called alkaline hydrolysis.

The big thing that's all the rage today is the funeral tableau. You can be embalmed and set up (as if prepared by a taxidermist) at your kitchen table, with a cigarette in one hand and a beer in the other, for your wake and your funeral. You could have them seat you on your motorcycle or in your car. All of these have been done. Anything is possible, and the crazier the better it seems.

If you do choose the cremation route, you can have your ashes mixed in concrete to make reef balls to help build offshore reefs. The stained glass windows at Robert Schuller's former Crystal Cathedral in Orange Grove, California contain the ashes of some of the parishioners. Or you can have your ashes made into a cultured diamond for your family to cherish in a ring or necklace.

All of these options simply trivialize the infinite value of the human person into, at worst, simply waste, or at best, a trinket, or the sum of our worst habits and passions. Who among us would trade his title and inheritance as Child of God, Body of Christ, or Beloved of God for a cultured diamond?

4.

A Better Way

Tombstones is my pillow, cold ground is my bed
The blue skies is my blanket, and the moonlight is my spread.
Early one mornin' death walked into my room
Oh well it took my dear mother, early one mornin' soon.
— BLIND WILLIE MCTELL

EARLY CHRISTIANS PERFORMED THE BURIAL PREPARATION out of necessity, respect and love rather than the requirements of the Jewish law. In both traditions, the person should be laid to rest naturally, in contact with the earth, with no mutilation of the body, no tampering with the remains and no handling other than respectful preparation. An autopsy should never be performed unless required by law. Hospitals will sometimes try to get the family to consent to an unnecessary autopsy. Some teaching hospitals have a quota of autopsies to retain accreditation.

When Elizabeth refused an autopsy for her 83-year-old grandmother who died peacefully in the hospital, the staff went so far as to intimate that Elizabeth might have something to hide. Fortunately, she stood her ground and would not allow herself to be bullied.

The deceased can in no way benefit from the procedure of an autopsy or embalming. It is not a sign of respect to mutilate the deceased unnecessarily in order to fill a quota or to make a lifelike mannequin of a person whom God has taken from this life. The family must balance their need to know with proper respect for the deceased.

Organ Donation

The Patriarch of Moscow has recently decided that organ donation is approved as an act of mercy. We have been registered organ donors for years. However, we're considering rescinding our organ donor status. The problem is that the organ donation industry is largely unregulated. Anytime you have large sums of money and little regulation you will have abuse. Organ trafficking around the world is huge business, often with ties to organized crime. Poor people are selling their organs, often being cheated in the process and sometimes losing their lives. Some of these trafficked organs have shown up in the United States.

Even at best, everyone in the organ donation industry makes a huge profit every step of the way. The only people who don't make a profit are the donor and the donor's family. The donor's family, suffering the tragic loss of an otherwise healthy loved one, is asked to donate, with no compensation, so that others may reap large profits. Somehow this just doesn't add up for us.

Our new forms in Appendix B now provide for "local only" donation. If there is someone in dire need at a hospital across town then, by all means, give them my heart. What we're opposed to is having our body parts distributed piecemeal through an unregulated system. Each of us must make our own decisions regarding this difficult issue. On the other hand, whole body donation is not allowed for Orthodox Christians at any time. The human body is simply too precious to us.

The Movement to Natural Burial

The memorial societies of the 1950s and 1960s were a reaction to the abuses of the funeral industry. Today, another reaction is beginning with the ecologically conscious Baby Boom generation and their children. Even in our self-absorbed age we can find a return to simplicity in funerals. The movement toward "Green" burials is making its way around the United States.

Much of the information that is available these days is decidedly "New Age," but the concept is remarkably ancient Christian. In a few areas of the country, people are setting aside tracts of undeveloped, often wooded land for preservation by designating them as cemeteries for natural burial. Americans' near obsession with perpetual care makes cemetery designation a viable form of land preservation. Bodies are prepared by families, friends or churches. A site is selected and a grave dug. Caskets range from beautifully crafted wood to quickly decomposing corrugated cardboard. They are decorated by the children with crayons and inscribed with loved ones' messages of love and loss. If a person desires a marker, a stone from the property can be selected and engraved with the name of the deceased. Grave locations are maintained by GPS coordinates.

Natural burial tends to raise questions about sanitation, the water table, legalities, etc. Many of these have been fostered by the funeral industry. There are no laws that prevent natural burial anywhere in the United States. You will have to check for local regulations. They may not be easy to find. Natural burial is so, well, natural that there is really very little reason to regulate it. Certainly there are some needs such as a Death Certificate, a Burial, Removal and Transportation Permit, and a Certificate of Final Disposition, to prove the body was buried and not sold on the black market or some such offense.

In order to understand the claims in favor of natural burial, it is necessary to understand a little of the process of decomposition. This is very common-sense and not too graphic.

First we must have a little knowledge of the human organism. Ninety-six percent of our body weight comes from organic elements present in many different forms. DNA, RNA, proteins, lipids and sugars are all composed primarily of oxygen (65.0%), carbon (18.5%), hydrogen (18.5%) and nitrogen (18.5%). Molecules of water (H_2O) and carbon dioxide (CO_2) as well as other smaller molecules are made up of these elements. Around sixty percent of our body weight is water, depending on the amount of fat in the body. Fat is only ten percent water. If all of the organics are taken away, we are left with around four percent, or five to seven pounds of simple salts such as calcium—the major component of bones and teeth—iron, sulfur and potassium. Other trace elements comprise less than 0.5% of total body weight.

As you can see, the major components of the human body are, quite naturally, the basic building blocks of life: carbon, oxygen, hydrogen and nitrogen; the most abundant elements in the universe. The other components are also naturally occurring and ubiquitous. They are in such small quantities in the human body that they could not possibly pose a health hazard. Indeed the recycling of elements such as nitrogen, carbon and phosphorus is an essential part of the earth's economy. Embalming and refrigeration interfere with this recycling process. Refrigeration, however, is reversible. Chemical embalming is not.

As we mentioned before, OSHA lists over 260 chemicals to which embalmers are exposed and from which they need to be protected. Quite simply, which do you think would be more environmentally friendly?

When a person dies, the individual cells do not die immediately. In some cases they maintain their integrity for several days. The first thing that happens when a body is buried in contact with the soil is dehydration. As the cells in the body die, the cell wall loses integrity and the water inside the cell simply drains into the soil. Within two to four weeks, what remains of a buried body is a skeleton with skin. A human body buried in a grave without any coffin or embalming treatment will decompose to a bare skeleton within ten to twelve years.

If the body remains in a sealed coffin, whether of wood or some other material, after several years it will become a moldy mass of unrecognizable remains with a marked odor of decay. Hence the importance of a soft wood coffin that will decay quickly. Burial without a coffin is still the best option. The traditional covering is a shroud or winding sheet. Sprigs of rosemary or other aromatic herbs are often placed on the body before enclosure. Rosemary is a symbol of love and remembrance and has the added virtue of a strong pleasing odor.

The issue of a memorial stone will certainly be left to the deceased or the family. We caution you again to do your homework and beware. Memorial makers have several tricks of their own. Mark has always liked the idea of an oak or walnut tree as his marker.

It is said that before the Battle of Bronkhorstspruit in the First Boer War (1880), the men of the 94th regiment raided a nearby orchard and stuffed their pockets and knapsacks with peaches. After the battle the dead were buried on the spot in their uniforms. Ten years later it was noted that there were "two uncommonly fine orchards" at that site.

Many years ago, a friend of ours told us of an ancient family tradition in the hills of West Virginia. He told us that his forebears were buried sitting up on the side of a hill facing east. In their breast pocket, the family placed three walnuts. We have always thought that is a lovely custom; albeit not strictly ancient Christian. The walnuts were to grow a tree for the marker. Three seeds are always planted in each hole in the hope that at least one will grow.

There are several sites on the internet where one can place a perpetual obituary at little or no cost. One could even, with very little effort or cost, set up one's own memorial web site for a loved one.

By and large, we Americans are simply terrified by the thought of death and dying. Most people do not wish to learn about how to deal with death until they are confronted with it. Then they find themselves at the mercy of those who deal with it every day for their livelihood.

When we are confronted with death, we are not inclined to study how religion approaches it. Rather than interact with the reality of death we tend only to react to it, often in unhealthy ways. Death is a part of life. Christians believe that life is a gift from God. Death, as it stands in opposition to life, and therefore in opposition to God, is evil and fearful. But as we shall see in the next chapter, God works all things for man's good and his salvation. Even death has become a gift of God's great mercy. Death care is quite simply an extension and natural progression in completing the cycle of loving Christian care from birth to the grave.

5.

Why Man? Why Death?

I want to know the mind of God.
Everything else is just details.
— ALBERT EINSTEIN

God in time of sickness
God in the doctor too
In the time of the influenza
He truly was a God to you
Well he's God, God don't never change
He's God, always will be God
— BLIND WILLIE JOHNSON

WHY DO WE FEAR DEATH SO MUCH? How can we overcome this fear? Why should we care about the preparation of the corpse? The answers to these and many more questions are contained in the sacred Scriptures and the God-inspired illumination of them by the Holy Fathers.

In order to successfully deal with death we must first overcome the universal fear of it, and understanding is the best cure for fear. To understand why we should care about the preparation of the dead for burial, we need to have some knowledge of anthropology, the Church's universal understanding of the nature of man, the origin of death and its defeat. This is not Christian anthropology. There aren't different "brands" of anthropology. There is only one, and the Church provides the best understanding of what it means to be a Human Being.

We will try to provide some admittedly simplistic answers to these questions and attempt to impart some appreciation of the flavor of the writings of the early Church Fathers on this subject and its universal importance. It is not possible to go into detail in this setting. Rather, it is our hope to encourage an understanding of the need for ancient Christian traditions regarding death and dying.

The Scriptures and the Fathers stand in direct opposition to the "spirit of this world." This is the same spirit by which sin entered the world and man chose death over life. We must educate ourselves and our brethren about the ancient Christian view of life and death and how to prepare temporally as well as spiritually. The Scriptures, and the Fathers' illumination of them, strain to educate and raise our consciousness from the lethargy of pleasures and entertainment to a true and deeper understanding of life and, of course, death.

All religions exist to help people deal with the mystery of death. They are all primarily about how we came to be and what happens when we're gone. Only Christianity reveals the truth about life and death and shows death for what it truly is, a great catastrophe and the great enemy to be feared but ultimately defeated. Only Christianity states unequivocally that death has been defeated. "Christ is risen from the dead, trampling down death by death, and upon those in the tombs bestowing life!" (Troparion of Pascha).

Christians of all confessions must strive to regain a truly Christian understanding of life, death and burial. The secularization of death, to which western Christianity is rapidly succumbing, robs life of meaning. The human person becomes just another animal, without virtue or any special role to play, destined to meaningless existence and eventual annihilation. We must resist this nihilism with true Christian understanding of the infinite value of human beings as created by a loving God, to live with Him forever in an ultimately intimate relationship of love.

True death is separation from God caused by sin and as such it is a great catastrophe which turns life into something God did not intend. Since this was not intended by God, it is not natural. This is the opposite of the secular belief that death is just a part of the natural order. Death is not natural. It is a terrible disaster from which God, in His infinite love and mercy, condescended to rescue His beloved. Only Christianity holds this hope and offers it to all mankind; the hope of resurrection and restoration to that ultimately intimate relationship with God in love.

Modern people look at death as a curiosity, not as hope. It has simply been reduced to an unpleasant but morally neutral event. This simply isn't true. Christians must understand and teach about the reality of death as the great tragedy of human existence. We must rediscover death as tragedy. Only then can we rediscover death as victory.

The Nature of Man and God's Intention for Him

It is only through Christ's passion that we can say any of the things we shall now discuss. In saying these things we do not discuss history as defined today, but we make a confession. We confess that Jesus Christ is Lord, God and Savior and that in Him we see the face of the Father. All of history springs forth from Him. The past, present and future point unfailingly to His revelation as God in His passion; to His cross.

The Logos (Word), Christ, was from the beginning the creative force of the Trinity pre-existing all creation. It is only in His passion, however, that He is truly revealed as the suffering servant, the Messiah foretold in the Old Testament. The Father, Son and Holy Spirit exist eternally in a relationship of ultimate love. Indeed, "God is love" (1 John 4:8).

Love is an incredibly powerful creative force. Just think of all the art, poetry and music created for love, not to mention the children. In God this incredibly powerful creative force deliberately pours out and is manifested in what we know as creation.

Man is the crown of creation, the very pinnacle of God's creative energy. God created man to live and converse with Him. Adam walked and talked with God in Paradise. He lived a life of complete communion with God. All of the universe was in balance, transparent to and filled with the Grace of God. The Garden is a beautifully poetic way of describing man and all creation being completely enveloped in the Grace of God. In this state nothing bad can happen.

God granted him dominion over all the rest of creation. Adam had the power to give each element of creation its identity, its name. There was peace and abundance, a life of joy and every good thing that God could give to man. Chief among these gifts was free will.

God wanted man to live with Him in a communion of love, not

as a slave or servant, but as His crowning creation. As such His love for mankind was and remains boundless. He created angels, powers, thrones, principalities and dominions to serve Him endlessly at His throne. Man was to be different, something special, above all other created beings. While the heavenly hosts tremble in the presence of God, Adam could converse with Him as a friend. God wanted man to return His love freely, and to that end He gave man free will.

Love must be freely given. God, as Creator who "is all and in all," gives His love freely. He does not have to, or need to. He does so freely. Man, as the creation, cannot love in the way that God does, but has the gift of showing his love for the Creator through the exercise of his free will in virtue and obedience. Man's obedience was the fruit of his love. Obedience that is coerced is not freely given in love, but elicited through fear or some other inducement. Therefore, God, in order to achieve a truly loving relationship with man, bestowed upon him the freedom to love and obey, or to deny and disobey.

Man was meant to mature into a relationship of total communion in love in the heavenly realm; a communion not unlike that which exists between the persons of the Holy Trinity, except that it was to be a relationship between Creator and created rather than the relationship within the Godhead. To that end, God bestowed upon man every gift He possibly could, even His own Image and Likeness. Through these gifts and this relationship of love, man was to grow into everything that God is, except that which He is in essence.

In order for this free will to be exercised and to grow to fruition in love, there needed to be boundaries of obedience and mortality. Man was mortal from the beginning. He was created in time. Thus, his potential to "grow into" the Image and Likeness of God. This is also seen in his creation from the clay of the earth. All material things pass away. He was a mortal being with the opportunity for immortality. God informed man that all things were his with the exception of the fruit of the Tree of the Knowledge of Good and Evil. Of this fruit man could not eat or he would surely die. This is done not as arbitrary selfishness on God's part, but out of love, for man's protection.

God wanted man to be free from passions and to live in virtue, free from care, with only one task to perform: to sing praises and to delight in the contemplation of God in love. There was no coercion nor any threat implied. God knew that the knowledge of good and evil would be the end of man's innocence and would bring the weight of cares and troubles upon him. God had this knowledge and, as a loving parent, He wanted to protect His children from these cares.

We fear death so much that it is hard for us to imagine that the mention of death was not a threat but a mere matter of stating a fact; just as one tells a child, "If you touch the hot stove you will surely get burned." The Fathers note emphatically that God did not say that if Adam and Eve were to eat of the Tree, He would "kill" them. He said they would surely die. He stated a fact simply and lovingly.

Death would follow disobedience as surely as day and night. Death does not come as punishment for disobedience. It comes as a natural consequence of man's choice to deny God's love, to disobey Him, and all the cares and troubles such knowledge brings to him.

Satan is jealous at the thought of man's growth into divine glory. The great hater of God became the hater of man. Through the deceit of the evil one, Adam and Eve were convinced that by receiving the knowledge of good and evil they would become gods and have all the knowledge and power that only He possesses.

Knowing the immeasurable gifts God has planned for man if only he returns God's love faithfully makes this first disobedience all the more tragic. Yet, man is deceived. Sin enters the world and, as a consequence, death is man's great unavoidable destiny; his constant companion.

Death was never part of God's plan for mankind. It is the result of a free choice made by man. As such it is man-made, and therefore death, by definition, is not natural.

After the Fall and Expulsion from Paradise

According to Satan's plan, death was the final punishment. At last Satan, the prince of darkness and death, finally had God's crowning glory under his power, and death reigned. Satan, the father of sin, the great deceiver even of himself, thought he had defeated God's plan.

In an instant, man was expelled from his intimate relationship with God and found himself outside His enveloping Grace in an alien and hostile world. Just as man is both physical and spiritual, so Paradise is dimensional and metaphysical also. Man cannot once again attain that state of Paradise by his own power once he has been banished (Genesis 3:24) (Hebrews 11:13). The hymns of the ancient Church express the great dismay of Adam and Eve weeping and wailing outside the gates of Paradise, where the gates were locked and guarded by the Cherubim and a flaming sword (Genesis 3:24). They find themselves in another state of being.

Adam and Eve's lot was exile; an exile that could only end in death. As we have shown, death was not punishment for sin. This sin was freely chosen, and its consequences were known. God did not prevent man from sinning. Nor did He punish him, in our traditional way of thinking. God simply allowed man freely to choose his own way of life. We chose to marry ourselves to material things rather than God and thus became subject to all the difficulties of material existence. This is the great catastrophe. We chose to separate ourselves from God. In this choice we lost communion with God and the potential for that ultimately intimate relationship with Him for which we were created. The rest of the Old Testament is about God setting the stage for His final victory over sin and death and the redemption of Adam.

Hunger and thirst, toil, deprivation and degradation are man's lot from this point on. Saint John Chrysostom points out that even these were not given to man as punishment but for education and amendment. For when Adam lived an "unlaborious" life in Paradise he fell into sin. But when the Apostle toiled hard day and night, then he was taken up into Paradise and ascended to the third heaven (2 Corinthians 11:27–12:2).

If there is punishment to be found in the expulsion from Paradise, it is in the separation from that intimate relationship with the Creator. This spiritual death—separation from the Creator, the Source of Life— is the only true death. This was the true power of death, the power to separate man from God. This pains God as well. What loving parent can bear to be separated from the children he or she loves so completely? Who among us would not do absolutely anything to restore them into our presence? In His great love for mankind God restores this communion through Christ.

Unknown to Satan, God in His great, unfathomable love for mankind, takes Satan's victory—death—and in His greatness, generosity and love, turns it from defeat and punishment into release and rest, awaiting the final victory. This is illustrated by the ancient Fathers, who point to the fact that Adam and Eve did not immediately die. God, in His exceeding goodness, could not allow His creation to be destroyed utterly and to disappear completely.

Adam and Eve were turned out of Paradise into toil and privation. They found their meager joys just as we do today. They knew the satisfaction of a summer rain, a good crop and the taste of it, and the birth of children; to us the greatest joy. Yet, to Adam and Eve, with the memory of Paradise and communion with God still haunting them, even children must have been a bittersweet joy.

Even worse, while toiling desperately alongside their sons, Adam suffers the greatest pain anyone can imagine. He must suffer the unthinkable horror of the brutal murder of one son by the other. Physical death does not enter human history with Adam, who "shall surely die," but with his beloved son Abel, in a most horrible and sinful manner. The Fathers point out that were it not for death, this horror, suffering and degradation would be man's lot forever.

We must not forget that in Paradise man was given dominion over all of creation. When God finished creation He set man over it all, and it was good. When man fell from the height of creation it was unnatural and the shock wave was felt throughout the whole cosmos. It resounds even today. The sin of man, who was above all of the goodness of creation, disturbed all that was good. The goodness and perfect balance of God's creation was invaded by the evil of man's sin. Nothing will be the same until the appointed time when God shall recreate and restore the former balance. All of creation is still good and gives praise ceaselessly to the creator, but like its crown, it suffers in travail.

Man was created as a mystical, harmonious union of body and soul. The body was created for the soul and the soul for the body. Man was whole during his time of innocence and sinlessness. He was created to grow into the true image and likeness of God in body and soul. Now, he finds his body at war with his soul. There is a constant struggle for dominance of one over the other.

This is the origin of all suffering. Everything from sadness to madness, from indigestion to birth defects and cancer is a result of man's decision to turn from God and trust in himself. But in and through Christ, even suffering can become a path to renewed trust in God. In Christ, suffering can become a path to ultimate victory, to eternal life.

In Paradise, all things are in balance. This is the "natural," God-ordained state of creation. There is no groaning of nature under an unnatural strain of sin and denial of God. All of creation praises God without ceasing. We praise God for who He is and the creation that we know, all the good things in it and all the joys of this existence to which we are so attached. Yet, all these must be very poor shadows of living fully within the Grace of God. One can hardly bear to meditate upon it and upon the loss of it.

Saint John of Damascus (c. 676–787 AD) says God did not disregard man but He first trained him in many ways and called him back, by groans and trembling. He inspired prophets to declare His truth even when we refused to hear. He saved man through Noah. He taught man humility through the introduction of many languages at the Tower of Babel. As man scattered and continued in his hubris, under the deception of Satan and the power of death, God selected a people whom He would instruct and through whom He would work His plan of salvation.

He spoke to the chosen people not as a friend, as he had before, but through prophets and the Law. He gave His people the Law to teach them humility and to provide for a prosperous future. "God earnestly strove to emancipate man from the widespread and enslaving bonds of sin … and to effect man's return to happiness," says Saint John. In His goodness He did not disregard the frailty of His handiwork and consider him a failure but, moved with compassion, He stretched forth His hand to him. Ultimately, He came in the Person of the Son to work the restoration of the human race.

The Incarnation — The Beginning of the Abolition of Death

Again, Saint John of Damascus teaches that "since the enemy snares man by the hope of Godhead, he himself is snared in turn by the screen of flesh." God accomplishes this, moved with great compassion for man, that in His goodness and justice, He would not, by His might, simply snatch man from death, nor give the victory to another. No, in His great wisdom He delivers a "most fitting solution to the difficulty." He bends the heavens to descend to earth, to take on flesh, not instantly or magically, but completely; receiving His flesh in His pure but human mother's virgin womb, with all the cares and travail that come along with it. God, Who is perfect, becomes perfect Man, the new Adam, that through the flesh of man and the power of God, the power of death may finally and utterly be destroyed. He made him who "had become through his sins the slave of death, himself once more conqueror and rescued like by like, most difficult though it seemed…" (Saint John of Damascus, *An Exact Exposition of the Orthodox Faith*, Book III).

When God the Son, the Creator of all things, chose to enter His own creation, He made all things new. The uncontainable One, who holds the whole universe in His hand, chose to lower Himself, to be contained. What greater thing is there than that God should become man? He chose first to be contained in the womb of a virgin mother and then, wrapping Himself in the garment of our own flesh, He chose to be contained within a body of flesh just like our own. He moved heaven and placed it in the Virgin's womb. This in itself is redemption of the flesh as God made our flesh His own.

His incarnation makes it possible that, "in Him," all men may live and become truly human, and once again become by grace what God is by nature. The promise of Paradise is restored.

Saint John Chrysostom teaches us that the symbols of our defeat in Paradise were the virgin, the tree and death. Eve was the virgin, for she had not yet known Adam. The tree was the tree of the knowledge of good and evil. Death was the result of Adam's disobedience. Now again we have a virgin, a tree and death; the symbols of defeat now become the symbols of victory! For instead of Eve, we now have the Virgin Mary. Instead of the tree of the knowledge of good and evil, we have the tree of the Cross. Instead of the death of Adam (separation from God), we have the death of Christ, the God-Man. Death was defeated using the same means by which it had prevailed: the virgin, the tree and death! Thus, the circular nature of all creation focused on a single point, the Cross of Christ.

Through His ministry, Christ shows God's continuing love for mankind. He illustrates the kingdom of heaven to those who would see, and He gives instructions as to how God expects men to treat each other. Through His transfiguration He shows His divinity and illustrates definitively that the soul and body continue on after death, as He is seen conversing with Moses and Elijah. He Himself is resurrected in the body, bearing all the marks of His passion.

Christ and the prophets preached repentance and a return to God. Yet, not even repentance is sufficient to wipe out the physical result of the first disobedience of Adam. Repentance absolves the guilty from his sins. However, man did not only sin, but through his sin he chose love of himself over the love of God, he chose death. Repentance could not conquer death. Saint Gregory of Nyssa teaches that, "As the beginning of death came through one man and was then transmitted to human nature, in a similar way the beginning of the Resurrection came through one, the God-Man, and then was extended to the whole of humanity" (Catechetical Homily 16).

Satan, through death, held captive the souls of all those who lived since Adam. He held them as "treasures in darkness and hoards in secret places" (Isaiah 45:3). But Christ came to save all mankind. The only way to reach them was to descend to them. The only way to do that was through death. Satan saw to it that Christ's death was perhaps the most horrific since that of Abel. The spotless lamb was led to the slaughter through deceit and treachery, to die the most torturous death yet invented: death on the cross. Evil presumed it had triumphed over the King of Glory when, in reality, it had only played a part in the glorious plan of salvation.

Saint John Chrysostom teaches that the only digestible food for death is sin. Though Christ suffered all the temptations of the flesh and spirit that Satan could throw at Him, He triumphed over sin and died a sinless death, without spot or stain. Hades received not another sinful man, but a new man, the only sinless one, the God-Man.

In His godliness, He submitted to the hate, scourging, humiliation and finally death on the cross, outside the gates of the city, with thieves and murderers. We see in this God's ultimate sacrificial love for mankind. In His humanity, He sinlessly submitted to the same degradation. In this we see mankind's perfected love for God. Here the two are joined and revealed in victory. Here is revealed the same all-encompassing, overflowing love that created the universe. This is the ultimate victory from which all of salvation, both Old and New Testament, flows.

Mankind was never created to be a slave of death. Christ, by being raised bodily, establishes how unnatural death really is to man. In all of human history, only one man, Jesus Christ, was created to die. Human nature, which, from Adam to Christ, was defeated again and again by sin, through Christ, received a unique, universal victory. This new man, free of spot or stain, willingly hated and sacrificed in love for God and Man, restored God's image and likeness and could not be held captive as His ancestors were.

Hell took a man and encountered God. Christ died and descended into Hell first, that "He might destroy him who has the power of death, that is, the devil," and to destroy and annihilate completely the authority of death and Hades. He preached the Gospel of salvation to those who, since the beginning, were captives of sin, in this way liberating and redeeming as many of them as would receive His Gospel (1 Peter 3:19—4:6). As sin is the only food suitable for death, Hell convulsed violently, much as creation had at the fall; and as Christ destroyed its power, it vomited out all those who had received His Gospel (Hos 13:14).

All the while, Christ also remained in the tomb. His divinity and humanity were never divided, nor were His soul and body. All this was accomplished in an ineffable manner. When He rose bodily, His Resurrection was the confirmation and fulfillment of His Incarnation as the restoration of true life to human nature and the final revelation of Christ as the Logos, the Word and Power of the Holy Trinity.

Christ was not satisfied with bestowing upon us only the gift of resurrection, great though it is. He opened the Scriptures to His disciples and showed them how all of the Scriptures refer to Him. After spending time with His disciples to assure them and emphasize that it truly was He, in His same body, who taught them and ate with them, He ascended bodily into heaven. He who bent the heavens and humbled Himself, without humiliation, to take on all that man is, then returned Himself and all that man is, now perfected, to be seated at the right hand of God the Father, in essence, taking us with Him. For He is the head, we are the body, and the one cannot be divided from the other. He moved heaven and placed it in the Virgin's womb. Then He moved earth and took us with Him to Heaven. He moved Heaven and earth.

With Christ's final victory on the cross the soul regains its purity and beauty, its former glory, and is made resplendent with Christ. With His ascension we are assured that, at His marvelous second coming, the body will also be resurrected, transfigured and incorrupt, much like our Lord's glorified body. It will attain the same glorious and incorrupt form as His and will live united with the soul into eternity (Philippians 3:21, 1 Corinthians 15:50).

In Christ, death lost its power, the power to separate us from God. It is fearful now in name only, not in reality. With the immeasurable gifts now bestowed on man, the new creation in Christ is much higher than the original one that fell. God did not simply restore us to the level of Adam before the fall but, through the resurrected and ascended Christ, our mortal human nature is honored more greatly than before. Saint John Chrysostom asks: "To which nature did God say, 'sit at my right'? He said it to that human nature which had heard once in Paradise, 'dust thou art, and unto dust shalt thou return'!"

By incorporating man's nature into His own Logos, the Head of the Church, God places him very much above the angelic powers and makes him a partaker of divine glory! Man, who through his own sin had fallen to such a low place that there was no lower place to fall, by God's grace and ineffable loving kindness, has been raised to a place so high that there is no higher place to rise. In the beginning the Creator made man in His Image and Likeness. Now He has united man to God. But for us to make the gifts of the Ascended Christ our own, we must unite ourselves to Christ and live His life as our own.

Death Before and After Christ

With this in mind, we must ask why we fear death so much. It is clear that, before Christ, death was truly an awesome and fearful thing. Life beyond death in the Old Testament was only realized through one's children and grandchildren.

Moses, Abraham and Jacob feared death. Jacob prayed fervently to be delivered from the hand of his brother (Genesis 32:11). Elijah became a fugitive and immigrant for fear of death. Job called it "the land of gloom and deep darkness." Joseph fell on his father's face and wept bitterly over him. There was great sorrow and lamentation for seven days (Genesis 50:7–10). The people of Israel wept thirty days for Moses in the plains of Moab (Deuteronomy 34:8), and all Israel assembled and mourned Samuel when he died (1 Samuel 25:1).

According to Saint Athanasius the Great (373 AD), "Those who would die were mourned as though destined to corruption" (*On the Incarnation of the Logos*). By this he means that the dead were believed to be totally lost. They ceased to exist and would never be seen again.

By the passion of Christ, death is transformed. Now it bears only the name of death. It is now rest, while awaiting Christ's return and our bodily resurrection unto life or judgment. The Lord himself called it sleep for his friend Lazarus and the daughter of Jairus, as does the Apostle Paul (1 Thessalonians 3:13—15). It is sleep in the profound and sure hope of resurrection.

While the aged Patriarch Jacob spoke to his sons of bringing down his gray hairs with sorrow to Sheol (Genesis 44:29) the Apostle Paul says that to die with Christ is incomparably better than to live (Phil 1:23). Saint John Chrysostom says that by virtue of the glorious Resurrection "the deception of the devils has been abolished" and "we can laugh at death" (*On Holy Pascha*). Indeed death is now so contemptible that many (martyrs) rush toward it readily and with joy, anxious "to be transferred to the other life" (*Homily 45 on Genesis*).

Saint Ignatius of Antioch was so sure of the resurrection that he wanted the beasts in the arena to devour his body and his bones. Biological death is not the real enemy. The real enemy is sin, which separates us from God. Separation from God, the source of life, is the only true death. One can be young, healthy, successful and be truly dead. Or one can be physically dead and truly alive in Christ. The main theme of the Epistles is resurrection. Christ is life and this world is death.

The early Christians saw Baptism as death to the world and the Eucharist as life and resurrection into Christ. Great Lent was the time of preparation for Baptism. Catechumens were baptized and received their first communion all on the same day, Great and Holy Saturday. This death in Baptism and resurrection into Christ is the beginning of Christian life. It is the passage from the belief of the catechumen, to putting on Christ in Baptism, to life in Christ in the Eucharist.

Life is fully lived only in communion with God as man was meant to be from the beginning. The Bible reveals that life itself gives the desire for life in God. The early depictions of Christian burial are baptismal images. The "last kiss" that we give the dead is the same as the first kiss given to the newly baptized. The catacombs, ancient underground burial places, are full of images of baptism and eucharistic images of banquets.

There are many more quotes and tales of the great martyrs that could be told here, but these will not answer the terrible nagging question: how do we overcome the fear of death?

6.

Overcoming the Fear of Death

Mother don't you stop a-prayin'
Father, keep right on prayin'
For this ol' world is almost done
Keep yo' lamps trimmed and burnin'
For this ol' world is almost done.
— REV. GARY DAVIS

Naked I came from my mother's womb,
and naked shall I return;
the Lord gave, and the Lord has taken away;
blessed be the name of the Lord.
— JOB 1:21

WE CAN UNDERSTAND WHY those who are far from the eternal truths of Christ are terrified by the thought of death. When our entire existence is tied to this world and the acquisition of pleasures, things and power, then death is the end. All is brought to naught. The long days of work, education, sleepless nights and struggling to the top of the social ladder are swept away in an instant like chaff on the threshing floor as we experience our last heartbeat. Little known to the unbeliever, his fear is justified, not because death is the end but because of the judgment that will follow. For the Christian this should not be.

The fear of death is cultivated by Satan, who hates man. Given the opportunity, he will so torment the mind with the thought of death, judgment and loss that it can drive one mad. More often, however, he uses the thought of death and our natural aversion to its evil to drive us from the truths of our faith. We become lax in our observance of our faith and in our watchfulness over our own souls. This weakens the soul into lethargy, to the point of seeing death as an hour of horror and suffering, and the judgment to follow as the terrible and unavoidable wrath of God.

Fear of Sin Cures the Fear of Death

The Fathers universally agree with Saint Isaac the Syrian (c. sixth century AD), who teaches that as long as man is careless and indolent in this life, he will fear the hour of death. Saint John Climacus (c. 570 AD) explains that "the fear which man experiences before death is a natural attribute which comes from the disobedience of Adam. But the terror of death reveals in such a person that there are still sins for which he has not repented and has not confessed and consequently has not yet received forgiveness" (*The Ladder of Divine Ascent*, Step 6, On the Memory of Death).

Saint John Chrysostom repeatedly emphasizes that our exaggerated fear of death is due to our insufficient fear of sin. We live a superficial Christian life. Our heart has not yet been won by a strong love for our Lord and the Kingdom of Heaven. The fear of sin and judgment abolishes the fear of death. This is what the great monk Saint Silouan of Mount Athos (c. 1866–1938) meant when he said, "Keep your mind in hell and despair not." He and the Fathers of the Church admonish us to ever keep our thoughts watchfully on our own soul, to remember the judgment and the torments of hell. In doing so we keep ourselves on the straight and narrow path and do not despair because Christ has saved us, and He provides us with all we need to avoid the fiery torments and enjoy eternal life.

As we try to redeem our own burial customs, we may be challenged every step of the way by society, by our own parishioners or by our own fears. Yet the recipe for overcoming our fears and temptations remains the same as ever: prayer, fasting, almsgiving, attending services, confession and communion, attentiveness to the condition of our own soul and watchfulness.

The Blessing of Not Knowing

Again the Fathers are in universal agreement that not knowing the time of one's own death is a great gift from God. If we knew, we might be more likely to be deceived by the evil one into doing whatever we please, because we could always confess our sins and receive forgiveness at the last moment. Saint John Chrysostom asks, if we knew the time of our death, who would practice virtue? Society would suffer from constant disorder. God wants us to be in a state of constant preparedness and ceaseless spiritual warfare. It is precisely because we do not know when the Bridegroom is coming that we must be prepared at all times, that He might find our souls awake and ready to greet Him.

God works all things for our spiritual well-being, as has been bountifully illustrated by the Fathers. If there were any opportunity for any good to come from knowing the hour of our death, He would not have overlooked this potential good.

The Memory of Death

The memory of death is one of the most potent and universally recognized antidotes for the fear of death. Imagine if we could live our lives every moment remembering that it might be our last, how differently we would live. The memory of death leads to salutary sorrow, leading to amendment of our lives, which leads to the memory of God, which leads to joy and gladness. The time for repentance and forgiveness of sins is now. "In all you do, remember the end of your life, and then you will never sin" (Wisdom of Sirach 7:36).

When the Patriarch bought and prepared his tomb in Hebron (Genesis 23), God no longer spoke with him as he had before. The Fathers reflect that the influence which is experienced by a prudent man when God speaks to him is also experienced through the memory of death. Saint John Chrysostom goes so far as to encourage us to pray frequently where the dead are buried, that the memory of the dead and of our own death might be all the more near as we pray to God. "Watch therefore and pray for you do not know on what day your Lord is coming" (Matthew 24:42, 26:41).

Why Is Proper Care for the Corpse Important?

The value of the body is immeasurable. It is the perfect dwelling place of the soul for it is into the nostrils of the material body that God breathed the breath of life. Man became a living being, body and soul united in the image and likeness of God. The Person, or Personhood is not found in the soul or in the body. The person is the unique combination of a soul and a body handcrafted by God for our salvation. In all of creation there never has been, nor will there ever be another "you." Even identical twins, who share precisely the same genetic makeup, are completely different people. You are unique in all the universe. Each one of us is loved with that infinite love that is the Holy Trinity, the love that created all things.

The real problem is violence. It is through violence that physical death became present, when Cain killed Able. God places great value on the blood of man, the physical body. The Book of Genesis refers many times to prohibitions regarding the shedding of a man's blood and to the related penalties. Proper respect was also shown for the dead. "Lay out his body with the honor due him, and do not neglect his burial" (Wisdom of Sirach 38:16).

God the Logos lived in a human body animated by the breath of God. He sanctified it and returned it to His Father restored and unblemished. Jesus loved, respected and cared for the body of persons who were sick, hungry or grieved. Much of His earthly ministry involved healing bodies as well as souls. It was through the works of the body—His miracles—that His power was made manifest.

Saint John of Damascus teaches us the body is so important that the judgment can't even take place until after the resurrection, when the soul and body are reunited. We are judged for what we have done, and all we have done has been done in our body.

The care of the dead is rooted in the Gospel narratives, particularly those relating to the burial of the body of Christ (Mt 27:59–60; Mk 5:46; Lk 23:53; Jn 19:40). Preparation of a corpse was so sacred to early Christians that they would rush to care even for those who had died of an infectious disease. The corpse was treated as a precious treasure. They would embrace and kiss it, then shut the eyes and mouth and carry it on their shoulders to be washed and clothed in a baptismal garment or a clean shroud. The care for the body was meticulous, sacred and respectful, giving great consolation to the bereaved family.

Saint John Chrysostom speaks of the anointing of the dead with aromatic oils and dressing the corpse in the appropriate funeral garments as one more sign of the love the community had for its departed brethren (*On Job*). The Fathers often speak of these customs, showing that, far from objecting to them, they very much approve of them. The great reverence and respect shown the dead is often illustrated in the Lives of the Saints. Preparation was considered so important that certain aspects were codified by Byzantine Emperor Justinian (c. 482–565 AD) to ensure uniformly proper practice.

What the Fathers greatly disapprove of is making a great show of earthly wealth or luxury in a funeral. Saint John Chrysostom writes extensively about this and about inappropriate displays of grief. Saint Basil the Great says, "It is irrational to adorn the dead and to do their funeral in luxury. So what is better? For those who live to be adorned with bright and beautiful garments, or to let these precious garments rot with the dead? What benefit is derived from an official grave and a luxurious funeral? What should be done is to utilize these expenses for the needs of the living… Consequently, it is better, before your death, to prepare yourself the arrangements of your funeral. A good funerary linen is piety" (*Homily 9 on the Wealthy*).

PART TWO

7.

Education and Flexibility

By medicine life may be prolonged,
yet death will seize the doctor too.
— WILLIAM SHAKESPEARE

Sound like I'm hearin' moanin',
Death bell all in my head
You know my mama told me,
Oh papa told me too
He said you know one day son,
That chariot, oh Lord comin' after you.
— LIGHTNIN' HOPKINS

WE HAVE GAINED SOME UNDERSTANDING of the history and theology of ancient Christian burial. Let us begin now to discuss the actual preparation of the body in the ancient Christian manner. There are numerous legal, cultural and organizational aspects to post-mortem care that we will discuss in later chapters. Education is the key to all our efforts to redeem the burial process. This educational process will be continuous. Success requires that the clergy and the lay leadership of the church be committed and involved in the process of educating and organizing volunteers. Ideally, this will become a commitment with volunteers of many churches working together in each burial society.

Completing the organizational process described in Chapter 13 will not be the end of the educational process. We will continually be educating medical personnel, nursing homes, hospices and funeral directors. Death itself is an evangelical opportunity. We have found that professionals who deal with death are pleasantly surprised at the love and care we show for our deceased brethren.

We have received excellent responses from observers regarding the power and beauty of what we do. Once educated, hospice workers are generally very happy to help in any way they can. A hospice social worker said, "This is the kind of thing I thought I'd be doing in my field. The reality is quite different." One morgue manager told us, "I've had Jews, Muslims, Buddhists, and Hindus in here but you are the first Christians." Even funeral directors have been touched by the love, care and solemn beauty of this act.

We are called to spread the good news of the one true faith. Fortunately, in America, no one can deny us our freedom to practice our ancient burial customs. Whatever others may think initially, if we take the time to educate them with care and love they will see the wisdom of our ancient ways. Let us approach each situation or objection as an opportunity to educate family, friends or personnel with care and love, rather than confrontation.

Most health care personnel are already familiar with the strict Jewish traditions and will be able to identify much of what we request with those traditions. When explaining to health professionals and even funeral directors what you plan to do, it helps to tell them: "it's just like what the Jews do." Armed with the proper pre-planning, we will be able to lovingly educate family and friends about the final wishes of the deceased.

Each situation will be unique and require the community to be flexible in dealing with different circumstances. Regrettably, not all deaths will be painless and peaceful, at home or in a facility. In the case of a tragic and sudden death, police, paramedics and coroners will be involved. These will be the most difficult circumstances of all and will require the diligence of the pastor, the burial society and perhaps the entire community. This is why it is so important not only to have parishioners' final wishes distributed to several family members but to have them on file at the church as well. If a traditional ancient Christian burial is the wish of the deceased, the pastor must have access to the documents quickly, to make sure the deceased's wishes are followed.

If this is not the case, often authorities will call a funeral director. If you choose to use a funeral director for some or all of the preparations, it is imperative that the funeral director be informed immediately, preferably in writing, that the body is *not* to be embalmed. Standard Operating Procedure is to embalm. This has become the base-line assumption and could be performed immediately.

In the case of a patient who has been hospitalized or is confined to home, a nursing home or hospice, it is best for the family to be honest with them about their condition. This allows a dying person to make medical decisions and express opinions and desires based on reality. These decisions could include treatment, pain management, "heroic efforts" and life support. Honesty also allows the person, particularly the believing Christian, to prepare for death. Psychologists have identified the five mental stages of death as denial and isolation, anger, bargaining, depression and finally acceptance. Honesty and loving support can help a dying person through these stages.

There is little anyone can say to ease the suffering of someone about to lose a parent, spouse, child or close friend. We enter each situation with fear and trepidation, knowing that each time we engage someone on a personal level, we run the risk of being insulted and unappreciated as intruders. Visitors can do no greater honor to grieving friends and family than to just listen. It is best not to intrude with false hope, trivial conversation or anecdotes. It is important to acknowledge the reality of the moment and to offer support and sympathy to the distraught family and friends. It is not helpful to hear that it was "God's will," "you'll have other children," "you should be happy she's out of her misery," "I know exactly how you feel," or "he wouldn't want you to be upset."

We are not grief counselors. We are just brothers and sisters in Christ and good friends in a time of great need. If they need a shoulder to cry on, a cup of coffee or just a companion in silence, be there for them. This is the obligation of every loving Christian.

Medical science has shown that hearing is probably the last of the senses to be lost. It is fair to assume that most dying people can hear us right up until their dying breath, perhaps a little longer. So say your good-byes and ask forgiveness before it is too late.

As Death Approaches

When caring for a patient near death one needs to understand that death is not really a moment, it is a process. In the case of the elderly or the critically ill patient, hospice will be a great help. Don't hesitate to have a loved one certified for hospice care. It doesn't mean you're signing their death warrant. Indeed, the increase in the level of care they receive may actually help them bounce back. Louise was certified for hospice three times in five years.

The patient will go through distinct steps as the body begins to shut down. Hospice nurses are trained to recognize the steps and will be a great help in identifying them and helping you deal with them.

First the patient stops eating. It's important to understand that this is very normal. This is the first step in the process of the body shutting down. Inserting a feeding tube or forcing them to eat is very much the wrong thing to do. Elizabeth thought that if she could keep Ella eating she could keep her alive. She didn't understand the process and, therefore caused herself heartache and her mother some level of discomfort.

Don't fall into the trap of thinking that you are starving your loved one if they won't eat. The body has many marvelous mechanisms built in. One of these is that, when the body goes into starvation mode, in this case voluntarily, it creates endorphins, natural pain killers. These endorphins contribute to the patient's comfort. Forcing food through a tube inhibits this natural reaction and contributes to the patient's discomfort.

At this point all of our efforts as care givers must be toward increasing the patient's comfort. This is palliative care. Many physicians and nurses now are trained in palliative care. This is not curative care but care focused on pain relief and comfort. It can involve pain medication, massage and sometimes just knowing what not to do.

Don't be afraid of the use of pain killers. Many of us are afraid that pain killers such as morphine may hasten death. This is not true. Pain management has come a long way. Palliative care specialists are skilled in providing just the amount of pain relief needed to keep a person comfortable without hastening their death.

All Christians would prefer to be able to pray right up to the end. The object of proper pain management is to relieve pain yet leave us conscious and able to pray.

When Elizabeth arrived at the monastery to be with Mother Leubov in her last days, she found her in great distress. She was dying of cancer and was in tremendous pain. The nuns were not giving her the prescribed dose of morphine because she wanted to be able to pray. However, she was in so much pain that she clearly could not pray. Elizabeth convinced them to increase her medication to the prescribed dose. Her distress ended fairly quickly and Elizabeth was able to sit with her through the night while they prayed together.

Eventually the patient will stop drinking as well. At this point it is critically important to keep their mouth and throat moist for patient comfort. They've already stopped drinking but caregivers can help keep their mucus membranes moist with special swabs developed just for the purpose or with ice chips on the lips and just inside the mouth.

For some people it can be very difficult to watch this process. Breath becomes very labored as the body weakens. Each breath becomes a struggle. We human beings are programed to fight for every breath right up to the last. It's a good thing too. Otherwise our species might have died out long ago.

When Death Arrives

When death arrives, the attending doctor, hospice nurse or Emergency Medical Technician (EMT) will pronounce the time of death. In some states, a signed death certificate is required in order to move the body. In others, the coroner will issue a Burial Removal and Transport Permit (BRT), which is needed to receive a Death Certificate. In our county the Death Certificate is needed to receive a BRT. Know your local procedures. Contact your local hospital's mortuary services and the county coroner.

The Death Certificate is an important legal document. Now often referred to as the Vital Statistics Form, it contains the name, the cause and date of death, and personal history information such as birth date, birth place, social security number, marital status and parents' names. It will be needed in estate matters and used by the Centers for Disease Control to track mortality rates and causes of death.

Survivors should carefully check all information on the death certificate to make sure it is accurate. Certified copies are necessary for a number of legal and financial transactions, so it is a good idea to request extra copies.

It is an awesome thing to be present when someone passes into the next life. They should be accompanied by great respect, prayer and love, whether we knew them personally or not. During and after their passing, the personal behavior of all in the room should reflect the highest degree of respect for the person and the bereaved family. Since prayers are being said, the highest standards of church etiquette should apply. Discussion in the room should be minimal and concentrate solely on the deceased and his/her personal qualities or funeral arrangements. The deceased body should not be touched or moved, except for his/her own honor, such as straightening or cleaning it or moving it only if necessary.

When death is expected the pastor should counsel the bereaved regarding the deceased's final wishes and make it known that the church is available to make the arrangements and care for their dear one in a respectful Christian manner. If death occurs in a facility such as a hospital, nursing home or hospice, all arrangements and the documents mentioned in Chapters 12 and 13 should already be on file with their physician and the facility.

We will assume that the pastor and visitation team have been doing their job all along and that these things are taken care of. If death is imminent, the pastor will be in attendance and will be in touch with the visitation team, prayer team and the preparation team. When we are notified that death is "imminent" this may mean several hours. It would be preferable to have the visitation volunteers there to support

the family rather than have the preparation volunteers waiting for
hours and then working through the night.

The preparation volunteers should be notified in advance that they
will be needed. In smaller communities, volunteers may have to perform multiple duties.

Volunteers should be present to assist in the prayers for the depar-
ture of the soul from the body, and the prayers for the dead. Then the
preparation volunteers prepare the body for removal to a place of preparation if necessary. There will be different arrangements necessary in
each case. Many times, if the proper groundwork has been laid, complete preparation of the body can be performed in the hospital, nursing
home or hospice. This can be an excellent time for non-Christians to
see the love and care we have for one another under the most difficult
circumstances.

As in each step since the arrival of the visitation volunteers, great
care must be taken for the bereaved family. They must be allowed the
time they need with their loved one. It is vital that the team be patient
and prepared to wait reverently and be supportive of the family. Do not
stand aloof and removed from the family. Introduce yourselves personally as members of the church who have come to be with them. Stay as
close to the family as their comfort will allow. Some families or family
members may desire your support, your touch, and a kind word. Others may not want any strangers around. We must be diligent in discern-
ing the needs and desires of the family at all times throughout the process. Don't discuss what you are there to do until the appropriate time;
certainly not until the person has died, in any case.

There may be others there in need of support as well. Sometimes
there is a long-time care-giver present who may not be a member of the
family. In their grief, the family turn to each other for support. This can
leave a care-giver in need of support, feeling isolated and alone, unappreciated for the time, care and friendship they gave to the deceased.

After the person has reposed, if their wishes are not fully known to
some family members, they may think they are waiting for the mortuary to pick up the body. That may be the case if you are working with a

commercial funeral director. Otherwise the pastor may need to gently explain to the family that their family member requested a traditional ancient Christian burial and that you are there to make the preparations. It is a good idea for the pastor or team leader to have a copy of the deceased's information sheet and final wishes on hand in case there are any questions. If a problem does develop, the facility should be helpful in showing the proper legal paperwork to any concerned family member.

Be patient. People grieve in their own way. The initial reaction of some may be anger and disbelief. Demonstrate your love for them by allowing them to grieve. At the appropriate time, the pastor can explain that you will wash and anoint the body in the traditional ancient Christian manner (much the way Christ was prepared), clothe the body and take it to the church, mortuary or home, as the case may be. Make clear to them that their loved one will be treated with love, care and respect and that they are welcome to watch, or even participate if they would like.

Some may want to be present to watch. Another may want to help with the readings. Another may want to be "hands on." The act of preparing the body can be a very powerful conversion experience.

We have been amazed at the reaction of families when we tell them what we are about to do for their loved one. We always invite them to observe if they wish to be assured we are respectful. More often their reaction is that they don't want to watch, they want to help. We have many beautiful stories of families participating in the preparation of their loved one for burial. In taking on this service they show the utmost respect for their loved one. We have received at least one convert due to this service.

Caring for the dead is an unusual and significant emotional endeavor. Each step and activity should be well thought out in advance. One will not be called upon on a regular basis to perform the tasks we are preparing to discuss. The need for advance planning, completing the paperwork and organizing volunteers to help with the arrangements will be apparent.

We will begin now to discuss specifically the handling and preparation of the corpse. We plan to focus on the ideal ancient Christian death and burial, which can be accomplished completely by the family and the church family at virtually no cost. Throughout this book we assume the ideal situation with the involvement of the entire church divided into teams. Reality may be quite different. The ideal may not be possible for you or your community at this time. It's important to remember that it only takes two people to prepare a body for burial. It's good to have a third person as reader but not entirely necessary. There are many variations on the "ideal" situation. There are no hard and fast rules. The only rules are a prayerful attitude and deep respect for the deceased and the bereaved family.

8.

The Initial Preparation

Nicodemus also, who had at first come to him by night,
 came bringing a mixture of myrrh and aloes,
about a hundred pounds' weight.
They took the body of Jesus, and bound it
in linen cloths with the spices,
 as is the burial custom of the Jews.
— JOHN 19 : 39–40

Lord in my time of dyin', don't want nobody to cry
All I want you to do is take me when I die
So I can die easy
Jesus goin' make my dyin' bed
— BLIND WILLIE JOHNSON

Risks and Precautions

A CORPSE POSES NO THREAT to the health of the living except in highly unusual circumstances. Much of what we believe about dead bodies comes from ancient history. We live with a societal fear and superstition that stems from the plagues of the middle ages and earlier. This and our media culture's sensationalized reporting of diseases and their dire predictions of dreaded new plagues have led to some powerful misconceptions about the common corpse. Some pathogens do survive inside the body for significant periods of time after death but the chances that a person who has normal contact with the corpse might be infected are extremely low.

Open wounds are the only real concern. Knowing the person's medical history or reason for hospitalization will certainly help in situations where wounds are present. In the normal course of preparation the participants should not come in contact with blood at all. The most prevalent accidental infection from the AIDS virus is by infected needle sticks. There are no needles used in the process of preparation. If the public health argument of the embalmers were valid, they might be expected to have a higher than average rate of infection with diseases such as Hepatitis B or AIDS. They do not. Their procedures most certainly involve the removal of bodily fluids and even organs. The procedures outlined here do not.

Corpses of those who have died from these diseases pose no particular risk if handled with adequate protection: latex gloves, masks, aprons and rigorous standards of cleanliness. Generally dead bodies are less, not more dangerous than the living. They no longer breathe, sneeze or cough, and therefore any viruses and bacteria are contained within the body itself. Since our traditional preparations require respect and avoid violation of the integrity of the body, the container remains intact.

Preparations performed in a morgue will require universal precautions, gloves, mask, cap and gown regardless of the deceased's condition. At home we are free to modify these requirements as appropriate. Some patients may retain fluids. Swollen bodies can have fragile skin and will often have punctures from IV's that can leak. One should wear gloves when handling these bodies. They should be treated with special care, minimal movement and adhesive bandages at puncture sites. Always exercise good judgment and seek medical advice if you are unsure. If you have great concern it may be best to recommend a good funeral director who is willing to prepare the body as we prefer.

In the event of a terrible accident you may be forced to recommend the family use a professional funeral director. Discretion is the better part of valor. We don't pretend to be professionals. Sometimes it's important for the family to have the professionals work their magic to reconstruct a face. This has happened to us once.

In the case of an autopsy there is no question. You should call the professionals. We have not been faced with this personally but we have consulted professionals that we trust. Without going into detail, the condition of the body after an autopsy is simply more than we could ever handle. An autopsy should never be approved unless required by law.

Initial Preparation and Moving the Body

If the preparation cannot be performed at the location of repose, then certain steps still need to be taken for removal of the body to the place of preparation. If it is a simple matter of moving the body to another location within the facility, the staff may do so without the need for any real preparation.

If the body is to be transported directly from the bed of repose to another place of preparation outside the facility, some things need to be taken into account. Again, the staff may be helpful and prepared for this. Discuss with the supervisor ahead of time what you can expect them to do and what they would normally expect the mortuary to do.

For an expected death the team leader should have done much of this already. It is always best to plan ahead, know what is available and what the procedures will be so that the team can do their work reverently without too much distraction or disturbance. Take your time. There is no reason to hurry either the discussions or the procedures.

If any family members are there to observe, it will help their comfort level to see planning and quiet confidence. Have a team leader and follow instructions. If there are any comments, improvements or problems to address, review them later. This is not the time. The staff will also appreciate the professionalism.

When everything is ready and the family have left—or decided to stay, as the case may be—place the icon or cross from your kit at or near the head of the deceased, light a votive candle, charcoal and incense if appropriate. Begin with the prayer for guidance and help for the team and any family present as shown in chapter 14, and then read the Psalms, hymns and prayers which follow.

At the time of death, all the muscles in the body relax and any fluids in the bladder and bowel which are retained by these muscles may be allowed to flow out of the body. Stomach contents may be regurgitated and semen may flow out. One should expect this in differing degrees in each case. You can massage the abdomen and bladder area to facilitate this release. It will be easier for the material to drain at this time and it will save leakage as the body is transported to the place of preparation. Make sure that a diaper and absorbent material are in place.

When people die of natural causes the body has already gone through the process of shutting down mentioned earlier. First they stop eating and then they stop drinking. There is usually very little if any fluid left in the bladder or intestines. We have never seen much, if any, fluid release during preparation.

We all have a gag reflex. Whether you know it or not, you have one too. There is nothing you can do about it, it's a reflex. Mark's just happens to be bed sores. He can handle just about anything else but bed sore odor will trigger his gag reflex. Because of this, we now keep a small jar of menthol rub in our kit. A small dab of menthol gel on the upper lip is enough to calm his reflex.

Rigor Mortis begins in small muscles, face, hands and feet in one to four hours. In the large muscles of the legs, arms and abdomen it will usually take around four to six hours to begin. If you should encounter a body in rigor, massaging the muscles will usually help them to loosen enough to position the body. People who are bedridden for an extended period usually end up in a fetal position. Massage will also help here to relax the muscles and straighten the limbs. After thirty-six to forty-eight hours the muscles begin to relax again and some attention may be needed to maintain the position of the limbs, mouth, etc.

Moving a body is not terribly difficult if proper preparations are made, but one can be injured if proper body mechanics are not maintained. Take care not to injure yourself. Ask for help. If the person has been bedridden for a period of time, the staff will already have made arrangements for manipulating and moving the patient in the bed without incurring injury. These methods may vary by facility so discuss with the staff what their procedures and precautions are. If there is no provision made by the staff or if the apparatus has been removed, you can ask that they they return it or one can easily improvise. We recommend you always use at least two people to move or roll a body. You will find the following method, which we have used many times, helpful in a home environment as well.

Take a bed sheet and fold its length-wise dimension twice to about three feet. Your folded sheet now should be about three feet wide and the length should be the original width of the sheet. This is your "draw" sheet. The draw sheet is placed under the body and used to roll or move the body as needed. Roll the folded sheet until it is half the width of the bed. Cross the deceased's far leg over the near one. Taking care to keep your own back straight and using good body mechanics, grasp the deceased's far arm at the arm pit or shoulder and the far leg just below the buttocks. Lean backward using your body weight (not your back) and roll the body toward you. A second team member can help with this, pushing from the opposite side. Then the team member on the opposite side will place the rolled end of the sheet under the back and buttocks leaving the unrolled portion on their side of the bed. Slowly and carefully help the body return to lying on its back. Now repeat this from the other side of the bed. Cross the legs and roll the shoulders and buttocks until the body is on the other side. If you pushed the roll of the sheet in well it will be visible. If not, reach in under the body and pull the roll toward you, unrolling it. Carefully help the body to return to its original position on its back.

You will now use the draw sheet to roll, move and lift the body as needed. When rolling the body, don't use the draw sheet to lift from your side of the bed, putting strain on your back. Reach across the body to the other side and, with your back straight, use your body weight, not your back muscles, to draw the body over. This helps avoid injury.

Remove soiled bedding in the same way; rolling it up under the body and then pulling it out the other side. New bedding is installed in the same manner and, if possible, at the same time. Always try to avoid moving the body any more than absolutely necessary. Remove the deceased's pajamas or bed clothes. These can be cut off with scissors.

It is a good idea to place one or two disposable bed pads under the buttocks, on top of the sheet. These bed pads are designed to prevent soiling the bed linens. They are quite absorbent and disposable. You have a few in your kit. Now you can remove any additional clothing and diapers. Use scissors to cut them off if necessary.

Any soil from body fluids should be removed from the body at this time. Since the body is being moved for preparation it is not necessary to do a thorough cleaning, but the deceased should be acceptably clean before being moved. It will be an on-site decision whether wet wipes or warm soapy water are needed. Keep the body respectfully covered at all times. We will go into more detail in the next chapter when we discuss the final preparation of the body.

Put on a disposable diaper in the same way you placed the sheet under the body. You have at least one of the proper size in your kit (Appendix A). Regardless of the condition of the deceased, use the diaper. Moving the body can cause more fluids to leak out of every orifice. Place cotton in the ears, mouth and nostrils. Take care to be respectful and caring with all these preparations. Move slowly, talk softly and respectfully. Don't hurry the process.

The first thing to do upon death is close the eyes. In ancient times, this duty was reserved for the family. If they will not stay closed, place a small Q-tip sized piece of cotton, rolled to a slender length under each eye lid. This will usually help keep the eyes closed and looks quite natural. If it's noticeable you used too much. If you prefer, you can use an eye pillow or a fabric bag filled with rice (bean bag) laid over the eyes to hold them shut for a few hours until rigor sets in. We also find that just a very slight opening of the lids looks quite natural.

It is very important to get the mouth closed as soon as possible. There are two methods generally used to accomplish this. The traditional Byzantine method was to bind the mouth closed with a length of ribbon or scarf wrapped around the chin and the top of the head. You may choose to place a small pillow under the chin. Leaving the mouth slightly open also looks very natural. There are other methods to close the mouth more permanently that we will discuss in the next chapter.

Next, position the head and limbs. This practice was considered so important during the Byzantine era that rules for positioning the body were finally codified by Emperor Justinian. Evidently, people had become lax in taking the expected care in positioning the body.

Bind the feet together with a length of bandage and place the hands in the position they will be in for burial. Bind the hands together or to the sides temporarily so that they will not move around during transport. Remove the bed pads. If you have had to use warm soapy water to clean the body you may need to change all the linen. If not, leave the draw sheet in place and fold it over the body. Cover the body in a sheet or prepared shroud and tuck it in under the body. Lift the sides and corners of the clean bed linen that you installed along with the draw sheet and wrap the body in it.

If the body is to be moved to a gurney for transport, take advantage of any apparatus or help the facility or mortuary will provide. If a mortuary is involved, you can turn the body over to them at this point. If you have no help at all, you can install another draw sheet under the back, shoulders and head. Four people should be able to move the body to the gurney in this manner. Use as many people as possible and do a test lift if necessary. Place a pillow or pad under the head and shoulders to keep them elevated and minimize leakage.

If there are only two people and no apparatus, you can improvise a stretcher with two sturdy poles and two new, well-made, extra-large T-shirts. Simply insert the poles through the arms of the T-shirts with the bottoms of the shirts toward the middle and slightly overlapped. To prevent the legs from dangling, you may want to use three or four T-shirts, depending on the size of the body. You now have a stretcher which two people can use to lift and move the average body to a table or gurney.

Transportation

If a mortuary is involved they will transport the body to the mortuary. You can make arrangements to meet them to continue the complete preparation, or request that they refrigerate the body until your team can return to complete preparation. Regardless, the body will be just fine for 24 to 48 hours without refrigeration. It is good, in any case, for a team member and any family member who so desires, to accompany the body to the mortuary, continuing the reading of the Psalms until the body is reverently placed into storage.

You can rent a cargo van or hire a mortuary for transportation only. You can also hire a transportation company. These are the people the funeral directors call. Cutting out the middle man can save up to ninety percent. They will take the body to the church or other place of preparation. There can be many levels of cooperation with your local funeral directors. Often hospitals are not accustomed to releasing a body to anyone but a licensed funeral director. Patience, planning, education and the correct paperwork will overcome this. Do your homework and know the protocols of the facilities to which you are likely to be called.

If there is no mortuary involved, then transportation is entirely in your hands. Forming a transportation team relieves the preparation team of this concern. In any case, the transport should take into account the wishes of the deceased, the Church's respect for the departed and the sensibilities of the bereaved family. A cargo van, minivan or station wagon is perfectly suitable.

9.

Final Preparation of the Body for Burial

The women who had come with him from Galilee followed, and saw the tomb, and how his body was laid; then they returned, and prepared spices and ointments. On the Sabbath they rested according to the commandment. But on the first day of the week, at early dawn, they went to the tomb, taking the spices which they had prepared. —LUKE 23 : 55–24:1

The white funeral cloth and the new clothing with which the dead are dressed symbolize the new garment of incorruption. — SAINT JOHN CHRYSOSTOM

THE PROCEDURE TO COMPLETE the preparation of the body is much the same as that already discussed for transporting the corpse. It is much more thorough and comprehensive and includes dressing the body to lie in repose in the church.

The Service of Preparation in chapter 14 was compiled for use during the final preparation of the body and can be abbreviated for the preparation for transport. In practice you may go straight to the final preparation with no initial preparation at all. If no one is available to read the service, you might create a recording of the readings and prayers, purchase a recording of the psalms, or play a recording of liturgical music. Remember, it only takes two people to prepare a body for burial. We suggest that you limit the number to five people in the room at a time.

It is important to maintain proper reverence and respect. Talking should be kept to an absolute minimum. Be attentive to the readings and pray the prayers mentally with the reader while working. Set up the icon or cross, candles and incense as mentioned earlier. Preparation begins after the Prayer Before Commencing. The reader continues the readings (chapter 14) as the volunteers begin their work.

These preparations can be performed almost anywhere. We've prepared bodies in their home, in a funeral home and the hospital morgue. It could just as easily be done in the church parish hall. If you are in a hospital or a morgue you may be expected to observe Universal Precautions. You will wear gloves, a mask, hair cover, booties on your feet and a face shield. These are the rules and we always abide by them.

Find a flat surface such as a table or board to perform the preparation. It should be at about counter top height to maintain proper body mechanics, so you are not injured and also to facilitate lifting the body into the coffin upon completion of the preparation. A bed is acceptable especially if the person has reposed in the bed. If it is a hospital bed, raise it as high as possible. You may then lower it to facilitate placing the body in the coffin. The body should never be moved unnecessarily. Always remember that we are serving a member of the body of Christ. Since the body must be washed, you may place a plastic sheet beneath the body or the linens to protect the bed if needed. Often a person who has died in bed will already have a mattress protector on the bed. In that case the plastic sheet is not necessary.

If the body has been transported, unwrap it reverently and discard the soiled wrappings for new sheets. Remove the bindings from hands and feet to facilitate cleaning.

Massage the abdomen and bladder again before beginning the cleaning process. This may help prevent leakage while washing and anointing the body and while the body is lying in honor. Keeping the existing draw sheet in place, remove any absorbent pads and diaper and discard them.

Washing the Body

Begin washing the body with a good antibacterial soap such as those used in the hospital. It is recommended to use gloves while cleaning the body. For other normal washing and anointing it may not be necessary. Exercise good judgment and do what feels comfortable.

Disagreeable odors come from bacteria remaining in the body and from the release of gases built up in the process of putrefaction that begins in the abdomen. This process usually takes three or four days but it is another reason to evacuate as much of the bowels and bladder as possible. The other source of unpleasant odors is bacteria present on the skin. A good washing, therefore, is not just to remove soil but to kill odor-causing bacteria.

Do Not Use Alcohol. Remember, we have candles burning nearby. We don't want to start any fires, and alcohol burns invisibly. A good bacterial soap and warm water in a plastic basin is all you need.

Have a plan for this. Act purposefully and reverently in every motion. Cover the body with a clean sheet and uncover only the part of the body being cleaned or anointed. Start by rolling the body on one side to clean the back from top to bottom. Dry the back and then lay the body flat again. Change the water in your basin and start again at the face and work your way to the feet. Wash one limb at a time. Clean under the nails and clip and file them if needed. Nail polish is not appropriate. Change the water as often as needed. Be especially thorough at the buttocks and genital areas where seeping has occurred as these are the areas where odors will begin. Remember, this body belongs to a child of God who is newly born into the kingdom of heaven. Take your time and do the job as you would with your own newborn child.

If necessary, use the draw sheet to lift and move the body until the head is over the edge of the table. Hold a basin under the head and wash the hair as you would one who is bedridden. Blow dry and style the hair to the deceased's personal preference or leave it combed naturally and neatly. You may remove any wet sheets and replace wet draw sheets with dry ones for the anointing. Very often new sheets are not necessary.

Now is a good time to seal all bodily orifices. You have cotton balls and tampons for this purpose. If the family is present you may want to wait until everything else is finished and ask them to leave the room. Using tweezers, cotton can be placed so far into the ear canal that it will not be seen. Pack it full, gently tugging on the earlobe to straighten the canal.

It can take a good bit of cotton to fill the sinuses. We found very long tweezers, about twelve inches long, at the kitchen store which are perfect for this. When ears and nose are full, you can remove a little cotton so that it isn't visible. Leakage probably will not be a problem. After ten years and dozens of bodies we've never had a problem with leakage. Just be diligent in watching to see if this minor problem develops and deal with it so as not to dishonor the deceased or embarrass the family.

Tampons come with their own applicator and are perfect for placement in the anus and vagina. If you think you'll need them coat them with petroleum jelly before inserting. We still carry tampons with us though we rarely use them. We have never had a problem with leakage or odor. Only when a body seems particularly prone to leakage do we resort to tampons and that has only happened twice. We always use sanitary pads and diapers just in case.

Put on a new diaper at this time to avoid moving the body again just for this purpose. Use of a diaper is not at all disrespectful as it prevents leakage which could be embarrassing. Unlike the adult disposable diapers we use for transportation, cloth diapers, if you can find them, are only made for small children. You can make some larger diapers from thick absorbent cotton material, use cloth to create a loin cloth, or just use disposable diapers. The plastic in the disposable type will not decompose but otherwise there is certainly nothing wrong with using them.

Anointing the Body

The anointing is performed with olive oil mixed with essential oils. Essential oils are the extracted essence of different herbs and flowers. They are only to be used in diluted form. They are available in most cities at spas or new age shops that promote aroma therapy and over the internet. Since the mixture is for anointing the dead we like to have our priest bless it.

Essential oils are highly concentrated. Handle them carefully and safely. They should never be taken internally or used undiluted on the skin. Just as some of us are allergic to different plants, we can be allergic to these essential oils. Always handle undiluted oils with gloves, glasses and mask to avoid contact with skin and other tissues. Volunteers can test their potential reaction to particular oils by placing a small patch of anointing mixture on the inside of an elbow; cover it for twenty-four hours and then remove the bandage to check for any rash or irritation.

Some oils should be avoided during pregnancy and by those suffering from certain health conditions such as epilepsy or asthma. Because of this and the physical exertion involved in moving the body, pregnant women should restrict their volunteer activities to reading the Psalms and prayers. If any volunteers have concerns about the oils, they should consult their physician. It is not necessary that every person on the preparation team apply the anointing oil. The scent should not be so strong as to overpower anyone in the room. People who are sensitive to the oil may just refrain from touching the oil or the anointed body.

Always store essential oils of any dilution out of the reach of young children. They can be poisonous if ingested and they have an attractive smell. Treat them as you would any other household chemical or medicine. Remember, we are using olive oil, and essential oils are also flammable. Make certain that your votive candles are in a secure location far enough away from the body so that there can be no accidents.

Some essential oils are quite dangerous and should not be used in any case. Lists of these exotics can be obtained on the internet, at the library or from your local aroma therapist. We recommend that you stick to the basics of Frankincense, Myrrh, Sandalwood or perhaps even Rosemary. The first three oils appear to be relatively safe if handled properly. Their scents are also believed by aroma therapists to relieve some emotional conditions related to funerals such as depression, anxiety and stress. Frankincense has the added benefit of being what perfumers call a "base note." It has the ability to maintain its scent over several days. Rosemary herb was often placed in the coffin in the past as a sign of love and respect as well as for its scent. *Caution*: undiluted Rosemary essential oil is a neurotoxin and should be avoided during pregnancy and by epileptics. Again, always handle all essential oils with care.

We are using scents to anoint the body for the same reason the ancient Jews and Christians did—to mask odors. The tradition of pungent flowers surrounding the coffin at funerals arose for the same reason. The scent from the oil should not be overpowering. There is always the possibility that someone in the family or in the church will be allergic to whatever scent is used. Some people are very allergic to lilies, the traditional funeral flower, because they are so pungent. Here in the South we have several wonderful eucalyptus trees from which we often take cuttings for church. Some people, however, are very allergic to eucalyptus.

Essential oils should be mixed with the carrier oil and highly diluted. Olive oil is not a favorite of aroma therapists because it has its own odor that can compete with or sometimes overpower the scent. Therefore, the use of Virgin, not Extra Virgin olive oil is preferred. Virgin olive oil has been filtered, has a lighter color and less odor. The carrier oil carries the essential oil onto the skin. It also moisturizes the skin and encapsulates the essential oil, retarding evaporation.

The essential oils should be acceptable in a four percent mix with olive oil. Use four drops per ten milliliters of olive oil or approximately 120 drops to make eight ounces of anointing oil. Four ounces is enough oil to anoint one adult body. This is just a starting point. You will find what is most satisfactory and works best for you. Oils can even be blended together as perfumers do, but that is entirely up to you. If you would like to experiment there is plenty of information available to work with. Store your anointing oil in a dark plastic pharmacy bottle with a safety cap out of sunlight.

Apply the anointing oil thoroughly and liberally from head to toe. This may be done by hand or with gloves, cotton pad or sponge. We prefer to use the same sponges we used for washing. You can use new ones if you prefer. Also apply it to the face and back. Applying it to the hair is optional. If the face is disagreeably shiny while lying in repose in the church, gently remove the excess oil with a cotton pad, sponge or cloth.

We have our anointing oil blessed so we don't just throw the sponges away. We take them home and dry them outside and then burn them.

There is something truly remarkable about the effect olive oil has on the skin. When we first approach a body for preparation the pallor of death is evident. Touching a body at room temperature is still a bit of a shock. When we finish washing, anointing and dressing them there is a remarkable transformation. We use no makeup or hair products but they look like themselves again. It's hard to explain, but it really is a remarkable transformation.

Over the years we have tried several methods to close the mouth. In addition to those already mentioned we've also tried denture adhesive. Surprisingly few people's teeth actually meet. We've found one method that works every time, super glue. We were very hesitant to try it the first time, but after years of trying other methods we decided it was the last resort. It works beautifully. Just place one small drop just inside on the back top of the lower lip. Gently and naturally close the mouth until the lips touch and hold it for a minute or so. Be careful though. Super glue is visible when it dries and it can't be removed from skin. Take care to place it so it will only touch on the inside of the lips and not be visible. It will work fine.

If you need to remove a ring you can add a ring cutter to your kit or you can use a little trick we've learned. Wind dental floss closely starting at the top of the knuckle that the ring won't go over. As you wind it tightly around the finger the blood and fluids will be pushed under the ring and back into the hand. When you reach the ring, thread the floss under the ring and out the back side. Coat the dental floss with petroleum jelly or anointing oil. Now, ease the ring up onto the floss covered finger and, pulling the floss forward from behind the ring, slide the ring off.

Dressing the Body

Dressing the body can be a challenge because of rigor mortis and the type of clothes specified in the deceased's final wishes. The traditional ancient Christian burial attire is a white burial robe or baptismal garment. Burial shrouds are available from monasteries or other suppliers on the internet. The shrouds are imprinted or embroidered with the cross, spear and sponge. Traditional white shrouds symbolize purity, humility and dignity. Baptismal robes have no pockets in which to carry earthly wealth.

Clothing made for bedridden patients and that supplied by funeral directors opens at the back, rather than the front, to facilitate dressing. Dressing will be more difficult but still possible with regular street clothes. The easiest way to handle street clothes is to button or zip them in the front and cut with scissors to open the back up to the collar. After dressing, a few well-placed safety pins will remove wrinkles and keep the front from bulging. This is another good reason to use the traditional baptismal robe and shroud. Another tradition is a headband bearing an inscription based on the thrice holy hymn heard eternally at the throne of God: "Holy, Holy, Holy" (Isaiah 6:3; Revelation 4:8). The headband says "Holy God, Holy Mighty, Holy Immortal," known in the Orthodox tradition as the Trisagion (thrice holy) Prayer.

If one chooses the traditional shroud or baptismal garment, slippers, sandals or bare feet are quite appropriate. In any case, the burial clothes should be simple and in keeping with our belief that all mankind is equal in the eyes of God. There is neither rich nor poor; neither king nor slave. This is not the time for an ostentatious display of earthly wealth. The clothes should be appropriate to one who is about to stand before God, his creator. They should be simple, preferably handmade, white and perfectly clean.

By this time you should be quite adept at moving the body with the draw sheets. Cosmetics are not recommended but are optional for the ladies who list them in their final request. Unless they are specifically requested, do not apply them. If you must apply them, do so sparingly and tastefully so that the deceased appears clean and natural.

Once you've dressed the body it may be time to call for some help. If your community elects to have male and female teams, the ladies may want some help moving the body from the bed of preparation into the coffin or casket. It would be quite appropriate for the pall bearers to perform this function. Position the draw sheets under the buttocks and shoulders as described in the previous chapter. Have two people on opposite sides of the body lift on each of the draw sheets and one hold the head while another lifts the legs. The process should be accomplished without incident.

Alternatively, two men can usually move an average body as the funeral directors do. One man takes the legs and the other the shoulders. You can straighten the clothes when the body is in the coffin. Simply tuck them in under the body and make sure they're presentable.

Handling Dry Ice

Before placing the body in the coffin, place a layer of dry ice in the bottom. Dry ice is frozen Carbon Dioxide gas. It is extremely cold and should always be handled with tongs and insulated gloves. Direct contact with the skin will cause instant frostbite requiring medical attention. KEEP IT AWAY FROM CHILDREN. Dry ice does not melt from a solid into a liquid like frozen water. It sublimates from a solid state directly back to its gaseous state.

Dry ice is available from commercial ice suppliers, industrial gas suppliers and some grocery stores. Have your supplier cut thirty pounds into three chunks about two inches thick (ten pounds each) and two pieces one inch thick. It also comes in pellets. Either way will work.

It should be kept in a Styrofoam cooler because it will freeze and break a plastic cooler. Wrap each slab in a brown paper shopping bag. Dry ice will not mist if it is wrapped or covered. Arrange two of the slabs, wrapped in paper bags, in the coffin between where the base of the head and the pelvis will be. Break up the one inch piece, wrap it in a paper bag and place it on top of the abdomen. It can be placed under the shroud or clothing. The weight of a solid block of ice can cause an indentation in the abdomen which will freeze in place under the ice. Breaking the slab into smaller pieces and distributing it over the area can reduce this possibility. The head will be on a pillow. Remove the ice on top of the abdomen during viewing and services for a more natural appearance. We want to refrigerate the organs because that is where decomposition and odors begin. The extremities are not as important.

Any moisture encountered will be from a cold surface, such as the bottom of the coffin, coming into contact with moisture in the air and condensing it. Put a layer of insulating material such as a folded towel, layers of cardboard or crumpled newspaper under the dry ice to prevent this.

You will use around fifteen to twenty-five pounds per day or forty-five to seventy-five pounds for a three day vigil. Purchase two day's worth at a time. As the ice under the body disappears you can replace it with ice at the sides of the abdomen. We don't attempt to replace the ice under the body.

Store dry ice in the cooler, *not in the freezer*. The freezer is not nearly as cold as the dry ice. The ice will sublimate faster and its extremely cold temperature could cause your freezer thermostat to shut off the freezer. Fill empty spaces in your cooler with insulation or newspaper to eliminate air spaces.

A body can be kept by refrigeration indefinitely. With diligence much the same can be accomplished with dry ice. We remove the ice from the top and side of the abdomen for services and place it back, suitably covered, for the vigil and visitation. We kept our Archbishop Dmitri in the nave of the cathedral in Dallas, Texas, in August, for five days in this way. If the body was refrigerated in the morgue or funeral home, it will keep very well for a couple of days at room temperature with no ice.

The most frequent mistake beginners make is using too much dry ice. We are refrigerating the body, not freezing. If this happens to you, don't panic. Freezing is reversible, embalming is not. Just remove some or most of the dry ice and the body will return to normal overnight.

Transferring the Body to the Coffin

There are a number of ways to make the transfer from the bed to the coffin. Decide what works best for you. The funeral director's method of using two men is an option. Always be careful of potential injuries. If you have the manpower or the equipment in advance, simply lift the body while someone removes the preparation table/bed and moves the coffin into place. Another way would be to place the coffin perpendicular or at a forty-five degree angle to the body. The top of the coffin should be lower than the bed or table. Lift the body and slowly turn so that the volunteers with the draw sheets can walk down either side of the coffin. Lower the body and position it on top of the dry ice. Tuck the draw sheets into the coffin rather than trying to remove them.

Family members or others may decorate the inside of a home-made coffin. Simplicity is the key. There is no need for satin or silk. A simple white cotton sheet over some small white feather pillows placed along the sides to take up some of the excess room is fine. We are trying to use all biodegradable material. If you choose to do the same, plastic or foam pillow stuffing would not be appropriate. No lining at all is also fine. A bed of straw or reeds, fragrant herbs, eucalyptus or the like would be fine also. You can place flowers or fragrant herbs—such as rosemary, mint, etc.—around the body as well. Either cross the hands upon the chest or place them at the sides. Place a cross, prayer book or icon in or under the hands, according to the wishes of the deceased.

Elevate the head on a small pillow to facilitate viewing, reduce seepage and give a natural appearance. Remove the binding from the jaw and replace it with a pillow if necessary. It is quite common for the mouth to open slightly while lying in repose. This is not a problem as long as the cotton is not visible and the mouth doesn't open too much. If it does open too much, use the pillow to close it.

Since we have begun using super glue to close the mouth for every preparation, we no longer use cotton in the mouth and throat. The only place for odors from the chest to escape would be through the nose. We pack the nose and sinuses thoroughly so we can just leave the throat alone.

Clean your tweezers and manicure tools with hot water. In addition, we like to clean them with a commercial product called Simple Green. We've learned from our friends at the morgue that this product has the perfect ph to kill any pathogens we might encounter in the morgue.

Continue reading Psalms if possible while the body is transferred to the coffin. This will help maintain the proper reverential atmosphere during the strenuous part of the work. When the body is ready for transportation, stop all activity for the closing prayers.

These directions assume that the church community will do everything: clean, prepare and transport the body, build the coffin or casket, provide the flowers and readings. This is the ideal. Brothers and sisters in Christ should provide the final care for a member of our body. There are many ways in which some of these duties can be coordinated with a funeral director if necessary but, don't forget the basic services fee.

Coffins and Caskets

Coffins and caskets are relatively simple to build by anyone with basic woodworking skills. A coffin is the old-fashioned, six-sided polygon, wider at the shoulders and narrower at the feet. A casket is just a four-sided rectangle like those typically used today. Either of these can be decorated with a cross, wood burning, or even messages of love from the children and crayon drawings. There are several coffin makers on the internet. Some are listed on our website, www,achristianending.com.

We are partial to the coffin style. We cut a bunch of eucalyptus and put it in the coffin, close the lid and store it this way. Our objective is to have a coffin readily available for any Orthodox Christian who needs one. If they are so inclined, the family can make a donation to our church building fund in return.

Transportation

If you have only one reader, he or she may be quite tired by now. Someone else can take over if needed.

With proper reverence and care, transport the body to the church for the vigil. If possible, the Psalter reading should continue near the body during transport. Any mode of transportation will do. Uncle Russell was hauled straight up the mountain side in a 4 x 4 with wide mud tires. Grandma was hand carried all the way. Then again, our dear friend Jake, the ferrier, was carried to his final resting place in a horse-drawn carriage with a team of eight horses that stopped traffic on a four-lane highway all the way to the cemetery. You may form a small procession if you like.

10.

Lying in Honor

Return, O my soul, to thy peace,
The Lord has been very good to thee.
— PSALM 114 : 7

Lord, now lettest thou thy servant depart in peace,
According to thy word;
For mine eyes have seen thy salvation
Which thou hast prepared before the face of all peoples:
A light to enlighten the Gentiles,
And the glory of thy people Israel.
— LUKE 2 : 29–32

Arrival at the Church

DO NOT TRANSPORT the body to the church until you are sure you have enough bearers to handle the job carefully, without too much effort or injury. The bearers can meet the transportation team at the place of preparation, the church, or home, as dictated by the circumstances. If you are using a funeral home, they'll take care of transportation. In any case the ideal is to have the deceased lie in honor in the church, not in a funeral home. While this could be done in the home, as it was when Louise lay in our home, the family needs rest and a place of refuge. In the ancient tradition and in the Orthodox Church today, the church is the preferred location for the vigil.

Location of the Body

Eventually you may have a gurney or catafalque. Carrying the coffin will be fine if you have enough bearers to do the job. Place the coffin in the nave, feet toward the altar or pulpit as if the deceased were standing in church.

The center of an Orthodox church, in front of the Royal Doors is a place of honor. This is where the bishop stands to be vested before a Hierarchical Liturgy. If you are an Orthodox Christian and a layman, there are only three times in your life that you will stand there in a liturgical setting; for your baptism and chrismation, for your marriage, and for your funeral.

Your coffin maker can build a low, rolling table such as the mortuaries use; you can buy one, improvise, or build a simple X-shaped stand. We've been using one of these for years and we've never had a problem with condensation. A couple of our parishioners were antiquing one day and found an old rolling accordion type catafalque that a funeral director had discarded. It needed only minor repair so they bought it and donated it to the church.

Members can place a drape around the sides of the stand and arrange flowers around the coffin. Locate any floral arrangements as close to the coffin as possible. If the church or room is small, provide for cross-ventilation. It is appropriate to keep a censer burning during this period. We have never had a problem with odor, even after five days. We have performed numerous services with no odor at all. Be diligent and alert to any odor or seepage that may need attention. Keep the temperature in the room as cool as possible and comfortable. The person who mixes the anointing oil may put a few drops of essential oil around the coffin if needed. Replace the dry ice at the sides and the abdomen as needed discreetly between services or when other people are not around.

Other members of the community can decorate the church with flowers and tend to any other preparations. Remember that black is not the color for a Christian funeral. In the ancient tradition the deceased is dressed in white. This may be a sad time for the community, but it is also a joyous time, as testified to by the Apostles and all the Saints.

While it is important to bury as quickly as possible, Christians have no hard and fast rules about this as Jews and Moslems do. No state requires burial within twenty-four hours for an un-embalmed body. Refrigeration has made time between death and burial practically unlimited. Our desire for a short interval between death and burial is not about the body. It is about the bereaved family.

After Frank died our burial plans were delayed by just a few days. He was taken to a funeral home to await preparation in their refrigerator. He had lived with us for about five years. We had been through a lot together. Mark remembers that each time he walked past Frank's door he reflexively looked in to check on him. Each time he did that he remembered, "Frank's downtown in the refrigerator." The thought was very disturbing to him.

It wasn't until after the funeral, when the last shovel of dirt was placed on the grave, that it was over. Only then did those thoughts stop and life, more or less, begin again. It is important to complete the burial process as quickly as possible for the bereaved family.

In some way it is the prayers and the actions of the funeral that bring finality and reality to the death. It is a significant point in the grieving process. Without it, it is very hard for the family to properly process their grief and begin to move on. In the case of cremation, this simply doesn't happen.

The Vigil

The deceased should not be left alone before burial. In the Orthodox Church, it is our tradition to read the Psalter continuously from the time of death until the funeral. The reading and lying in repose will generally last at least twenty-four hours, so have plenty of volunteers available and make this truly a community and family affair. Don't let the visitation become a social gathering in the nave of the church. Everyone present should be aware, by the reading of the Psalter, that this is a time of prayer. The church can provide another room for family and friends to gather and reminisce. If the church is small, be imaginative and try to provide another place for this gathering.

Keep the visitation hours to the minimum so that the family does not suffer hours of trivial chatter in the face of terrible grief. With a separate room for this activity, the family can choose to go to either place as the mood strikes them. Some may want to stay and pray in the nave while others may want to catch up with family and friends in the other room. Some may go back and forth. The church should watch over these activities so that the bereaved do not become over-stressed. Have some ushers available during visitation times to greet visitors and escort them to the bereaved. Ushers can also inform visitors that there is another room available for talking. If family and friends want to continue with their reunion after the time allotted, they can go to an appropriate place.

Care for the Family

The funeral announcements prepared by the church family include the times for visitation. With the body at the church, there should be little disturbance at home. Be as involved as the immediate family will allow, remembering that our primary obligation is to allow them some peace from the very stressful time of the visitation. It only takes two people to prepare the body but there are many other things parishioners can do to help out. Church members can be at the house to answer the phone and questions. They can answer the door and accept food offerings from friends and family. The bereaved of the immediate family will need time to grieve privately and to rest. They will need this more than they know or will admit. We can also volunteer to drive them to and from the church and cemetery.

Many people feel obliged to entertain those from outside their home such as church members. Make it clear that this is not necessary. You are there to serve, not to be served. After all of our education efforts, this will become the norm and the bereaved will know what to expect from the community. Your efforts should not become just one more burden for the family to bear. The pastor should make it very clear from the outset what assistance the church family is prepared and able to provide and discuss these things with the next of kin so they understand what we are doing and why we are so attentive and indeed, at times, protective.

The Funeral

With no funeral director involved, you will need someone to take on his duties. It seems reasonable that the transportation team double as ushers and funeral directors at the funeral service. There should be one person in charge. The team's duties consist of organizing the pall bearers, closing the coffin, and transporting it to the cemetery.

The pall bearers should sit or stand together at the front so they have easy access. Members or ushers can remove the flowers from around the coffin before the service. We will need access to all sides of the coffin for censing and for the last kiss. The pastor closes the coffin at the appropriate time. Remove the pillow from under the head and under the chin as needed.

The ushers will assist the pall bearers in removing the body from the church. This is normally done feet first, so the coffin will have to be turned around. Place the coffin in the vehicle feet first, toward the driver. Your transportation team will assist the bearers in removing the body from the vehicle and carrying it to the grave. From the funeral to the grave site we chant the thrice-holy hymn: "Holy God, Holy Mighty, Holy Immortal: have mercy on us."

If it is a private or church cemetery, the coffin can simply be placed on boards laid across the grave. The grave opening should be lined by two-by-eight boards laid on the surface for the pallbearers to walk on and to prevent the sides from collapsing. At the appropriate time, the pall bearers, with the assistance of the ushers, can lift the coffin using ropes, remove the boards it rests on and lower the coffin carefully into the grave. This must be done in unison or the coffin could tip. Be careful about choosing the right people for this job. This will be up to the team leader at the appropriate time. As with all your work, these actions should be well planned and directed.

If you want to keep the ropes, the grave diggers will have placed boards in the grave to provide the clearance necessary to pull them back out. Otherwise just leave them in the grave. In the Orthodox Church, each person present places at least one shovel of earth in the grave. Let the family do as much as they wish. They can fill the grave or leave it to the grave diggers from the church. Often, at an Orthodox funeral, the family and friends fill the grave completely even in a commercial cemetery.

11.

A Word About Grief

Blessed are they that mourn, for they shall be comforted.
— MATTHEW 5:4

I reads the Bible often, I tries to read it right
As far as I can understand, a man is more than his mind.
When Christ stood in the temple, the people stood amazed
Was showin' the doctors and the lawyers
How to raise a body from the grave.
— BLIND WILLIE JOHNSON

WE HAVE TRIED TO PROVIDE A FLAVOR of the Patristic view of death and dying, in the hope of reviving the ancient Christian traditions of burial. We did not intend to discuss grief. However, the ancient writings of the Fathers we have read are full of insights about it. The Fathers and the Church have a deep, holistic understanding of the human condition and the stages of grief. They seek, through our hymns, services and life in the Church, to console and heal the bereaved. We feel somewhat compelled by the sheer volume of patristic comment on grief to offer a short overview.

"My son, let your tears fall for the dead, and as one who is suffering grievously begin the lament. Lay out his body with the honor due him, and do not neglect his burial" (Wisdom of Sirach 38:16).

Our grief is real and cannot be denied. Death is evil. It is the great catastrophe of human existence. It is not part of God's intent for man and therefore it is not natural. It is the result of deception and the choice of disobedience over obedience. The Holy Fathers teach that we must not be overcome by our grief unto despair. We must trust always and completely in our all-wise and loving God. They admonish us to use our grief for the profit of our own souls. They teach us that it should not be a shallow and superficial emotion of tears but a deep and abiding transformation of courage, contrition and compunction in the depths of our soul; leading to repentance. There is little we can accomplish for the departed now. The most profit to be gained from our grief is in our own repentance and amendment of our lives.

"That you may not grieve as others do who have no hope" (1 Thessalonians 4:13).

The apostle does not say "do not grieve," but only not to grieve as those who have no hope. The Holy Church has never forbidden tears for the dead. *Weep for the dead"* (Wisdom of Sirach 11:11). Christ wept over Lazarus. He did so modestly. We are expected to do the same with fear of God. The believer should express grief with propriety and modesty. It should never be extreme.

Saint John Chrysostom says that we should weep as though we are bidding farewell to a loved one going on a long journey to a far away country; for we shall surely be reunited there. Saint Basil the Great admonishes us to remain upright and above every storm as the wise and courageous captain is expected to do. The Fathers continue to assert that the Christian who mourns and laments "beyond measure" attacks himself. Dirges and wailing disturb and agitate the bereaved when the deceased has gone to calm harbors.

On the other hand our detachment from the reality of death seems at times to have driven us too far in the other direction. Friends and family seem to demand too much of the bereaved, expecting them to return too quickly to a normal life. We have lost most of our acceptable mourning rituals as well. Sometimes we feel pressure to return to normal, and guilt in trying to do so. The bereaved need time to mourn, and family and friends should be supportive and understanding.

Faith, Hope, Love Abide (1 Corinthians 13 : 13)

At times the Fathers can seem very stern concerning the grief of widows and parents. One must remember that in their time funeral processions of the pagans were extravagant in their mourning, with great shows of weeping and wailing. Great processions of mourners, some of them professionals, would fill the streets with people screaming and rending garments, wailing and moaning. The Fathers adamantly protested against these displays as belonging to "those with no hope of the resurrection." Since many Christians were converts from Greek or Roman forms of paganism, many of them continued their old traditional forms of mourning.

Those who act in this way are certain that the deceased is gone forever, without hope. They will never meet again. Their death is the end, total annihilation. Only Christianity, only Christ, offers the hope of resurrection and life eternal. The Fathers ask how we can convince a pagan of the hope of the resurrection if we too act as if we are as terrified of death as he.

> For sorrow results in death, and sorrow of heart saps one's strength. In calamity sorrow continues, and the life of the poor man weighs down his heart. Do not give your heart to sorrow; drive it away, remembering the end of life. Do not forget, there is no coming back; you do the dead no good, and you injure yourself. (Wisdom of Sirach 38 : 18–21)

To the Fathers, death is our passage to a brighter life. The Christian should face it with optimism.

The Death of a Spouse or Child

Christians see things differently from nonbelievers. Death is a sleep but it is also an awakening to the blessedness of the eternal kingdom. In the sure and certain hope of the resurrection, we understand that our unity and communion in Christ is perfected in Him. Saint John Chrysostom speaks of the blessed union of husband and wife being but a poor earthly and fleshly shadow of the complete union perfected in Christ in the kingdom. For then there will be "the union of a soul with a soul."

He poses a question to the young widow of a great and pious man. If her husband were commanded to come to the court of the king to accept great honor and to be clothed with finery and jewels, to return to her at some future time, would she then prevent him from going? He continues by expounding on how much greater the rewards her pious husband is now receiving and that they will be reunited in the palace of the King of Kings (*Letter to a Young Widow*).

He instructs those who mourn the loss of a spouse as their supporter to turn to God who is the supporter, savior and benefactor of all people. For those who have lost their protector, companion and consoler, Saint John Chrysostom teaches that God often takes our protectors so that we will learn all the more to depend on Him. Because we are rational beings, we must not be overcome by this sorrow, "lest evil change his understanding or guile deceive his soul" (Wisdom of Sirach 4:11).

The loss of a child is surely the worst loss of all. The loss of an innocent child is proof of the evil of death and that death cannot be part of an all-loving God's desire for mankind. Our Holy Church, as a loving mother, recognizes this and provides special hymns for the funeral of an infant. In this situation the Fathers ask us to think of Abraham, who loved God so much that he killed his only son. Even though his son did not die, Abraham had already killed him in his heart before he raised the blade. Therefore, God stayed his hand and rewarded him greatly.

Which would we rather have our son inherit, our property or heaven? We must remember that though we no longer have him as our heir, God has made him an heir. He is no longer co-heir with his brothers of our earthly property but is co-heir with Christ. The Fathers remind us that if we want to see our child again, then we must live a life of piety. We must remember that Christ died for us, but we only die for ourselves.

"The Christian believes that the all-wise and loving God knows exactly how to work things to the advantage of each person and why the span of our life is unequal" (Saint Basil the Great, Letter 6 to the wife of Nektarios).

Saint Photios the Great (820–891 AD) asks how it is that when a child is born we do not say that he or she was untimely born. When a child is born we say this is the will of God and at the right time, and we rejoice. When we mourn the "untimely" death of a child we depart from God and attempt to define the boundaries of life. To say farewell is always painful. The Church not only permits the expression of pain and suffering but, through her hymnography and prayers, also directs it in a manner pleasing to God and beneficial to our soul.

The Difference Between an Evil and a Good Death

There is no such thing as a good or evil, just or unjust death. All death is evil and there is only one true death, sin and separation from God. It is not for us to determine the timeliness or the worthiness of anyone's particular death. Nor is it for us to judge the ultimate disposition of their soul. These things we leave to God. No matter how cruel or unjust death may be, according to the Fathers, fear of it cannot be justified in the light of Christ.

Abel died unjustly but Cain lived as a fugitive and wanderer on the earth (Genesis 4:12–14). The one who died unjustly was blessed with his reward while the one who lived was cursed by God. Physical death is transformed by Christ into the eternal movement toward the blessedness of God. The only truly evil death is the death of an unrepentant sinner. We mourn for these sinners, not only when they die but also as they live. Sin is separation from God, and sinners, even though they live, are essentially dead, since they separate themselves from the source of life. The righteous, though they die, actually live, for they are united to Christ through whom all things were created. We should weep for those who are given the opportunity to be cleansed of sin and do not accept it. Even though he may have died with great wealth, it will not save him now.

"Precious in the sight of the Lord is the death of his saints" (Psalms 116:15).

We know that the dissolution of the corpse is not the end of the body, but the end of corruption. The seed in the ground has dissolved and is the beginning of the future harvest.

"I tell you this, brethren: flesh and blood cannot inherit the kingdom of God, nor does the perishable inherit the imperishable" (1 Corinthians 15:5).

Sacred Memorials for the Dead

The cult of bodily preservation comes from several pagan cultures that had no hope of resurrection and believed that the body was necessary for the enjoyment of an after-life. This is manifested in our culture in many ways, not only in bodily preparation but also in worldly remembrance and monuments. The Greek word for "tomb" itself is derived from the word meaning "memory." This is an indication that the body is lovingly buried and not simply discarded. But of what additional good can it be to the soul to have one's name carved in stone on a monument, no matter how impressive?

Many people work very hard to do something important for their community and leave a "lasting" legacy, like building a bridge or hospital. Of the millions of people who cross bridges every day, how many even know the names of the bridges, much less the people they are named for, their lives and character? Building bridges and hospitals is certainly good and not to be disparaged. However, as memorials, they are not permanent. Bridges and hospitals will come down some day and the large bronze plaques with the names of the people who worked so hard to make them a reality will end up as a museum piece or melted down.

Strolling through the historic cemeteries of Charleston, South Carolina, we see thousands of stones that are now barely legible, with names long forgotten. Even the poorest among us strive earnestly to have a monument by which our passing through this life may be remembered here. Strolling through any cemetery, we see only names; not people, personalities or character, and certainly not souls. Even so, some of us will save money our whole lives just to buy a beautiful grave stone.

Stone will erode and wash away in time. The walls and fences of our cemeteries are lined with old and broken stone memorials that are no longer legible and no longer mark even the grave to which they belong. Everything made by man must pass away.

The prevailing attitude of people, even Christians, from the earliest times, is to place disproportionate value on "lasting" earthly memorials. Christ, the Apostles and the Fathers of the Church struggled to teach the Jews, pagans and Christians about the reality of life, death and life eternal. They taught that the only truly eternal memorial is in the mind of God.

In the Orthodox Church we sing "Memory Eternal" at the funeral, at the graveside and in our memorial services. It is not that we wish for the person to "live on" in the memory of us mortal people who are also perishing. It is a prayer that they may live forever in the eternal memory of God. Saint John Chrysostom wrote numerous letters, commentaries and homilies on the subjects of death, grief and mourning. He stresses building up true memorials in heaven for ourselves and our departed loved ones rather than the earthly kind that pass away.

Prayer and holy memorials for the dead are as ancient as Scripture. The Israelites prayed to God to forgive the sins of their fathers who had died (Nehemiah 9:2 and 2 Maccabees 12:40–42). The Apostle Paul prays for Onesiphoros after his passing (2 Timothy 1:18). Christian love endures. It never ends (1 Corinthians 13:8). We are all members of the body of Christ. "Whether we live or whether we die we are the Lord's" (Romans 14:8). Saint John of Damascus tells us that it was the Apostles themselves who taught us to pray for the dead when they decreed that the faithful remember those who have fallen asleep in their services, particularly in the Eucharistic service of the Divine Liturgy. Saint Cyprian of Carthage (190–258 AD) informs us that early Christians considered prayers for the martyrs a basic duty.

Memorials for the dead are contained in each of the liturgies throughout the history of the Church. The liturgies of Saint Mark, Saint James, Saint Clement of Rome, Saint Basil the Great and Saint John Chrysostom all contain petitions for the dead. Saint Cyril of Jerusalem's (315–386 AD) "Catechesis" refers to commemorating the dead. The Apostolic Constitutions (8:42; third century AD) recommend that memorials for the dead be served on the third day after the death, the ninth day, the fortieth day and annually.

Every time we pray for each other we perform a holy act pleasing to God. It is our obligation to do so. The Fathers teach us also that the prayers for the dead not only benefit us, but that the dead also receive some consolation from this act. What form that consolation may take for an individual soul we cannot know. Yet it is clear from the Fathers and Scripture that prayers for the dead are very good and beneficial for the dead and for the living as well.

These are the true memorials to our dearly departed brethren. Saint John Chrysostom tells us that if we want to build true and lasting memorials to our loved ones we must practice virtue. Anything else will pass away, but virtue practiced in memory of the departed builds memorials in heaven that will not pass away. To Saint John the trappings of a wealthy funeral are derision and mockery to the deceased. The deceased is forced to bear "the symbols of wealth" and ostentation on his death bed.

Saint Ephraim the Syrian (c. 313–373 AD) requested that whatever would have been spent on his burial be given to the poor instead. Saint Anthony the Great (251–356 AD) left strict instructions that his funeral be simple and that he be buried in the ground, just like the prophets and Christ himself.

A proper memorial for the dead, besides our own amended and virtuous life, would be alms to the poor or an anonymous gift to the church. Perhaps one of the best memorials to all those who have gone before and all of us yet here, is to redeem the time, to practice virtue and recapture our own tradition: the act of mercy, the preparation and burial of the dead.

12.

Personal Pre-Planning

Do not lay up for yourselves treasures on earth, where moth and rust consume and where thieves break in and steal, but lay up for yourselves treasures in heaven, where neither moth nor rust consumes and where thieves do not break in and steal. For where your treasure is, there will your heart be also. — MATTHEW 6:19–21

I have a Bible in my home
If I don't read it my soul be lost
Father he taught me how to read
If I don't read it my soul be lost, nobody's fault but mine
Mother taught me how to read
If I don't read it my soul be lost, nobody's fault but mine.
— BLIND WILLIE JOHNSON

WE HOPE WE HAVE SHOWN that the proper preparation of the Christian body for burial is important. To the Christian, all of life is preparation for death, our entrance into the Kingdom of Heaven. The only real death is sin, for it is sin that is the destruction of the soul.

The things of the world easily deceive and mislead us. All our worldly preoccupations are fleeting dreams, which only mock those things that are truly essential. They are deceptive fantasies of the soul. As we deepen our understanding of this mystery we see that the things of this world are all earth, ashes and dust. We also understand who, among the people, are truly wealthy and who are poor.

Our attitude toward death is one illustration of the difference between those of us who believe and the society in which we live. It is an opportunity to show our Christian courage.

There are many facets to preparation for death. In this chapter we deal with the practical, legal preparations that must be considered, to ease our passing for our loved ones.

Part of the education process and preparation for death must be a certain understanding of the legal ramifications of our own death and the impact it will have upon our loved ones. In this area as well, we must be strong and diligent, as good stewards of all that God has bestowed upon us.

Who among us would not willingly die for wife or husband, son or daughter? Then why is it so hard for us to think ahead and make preparations to ease their difficulty, pain and grief at the time of our own passing? It is time now to die a little for them and consider the things that, often without warning, become the most important matters of the day.

We cannot stress strongly enough the need for each of us to complete the necessary paperwork as quickly as possible. Every heartbeat is a gift from God. We cannot force our heart to beat one more time so we need to be prepared at all times. We have been dealing with these issues for a long time now. We can tell you just how badly things can go if you don't take care of your estate planning and paperwork right now. It will cause unnecessary stress on your loved ones at the worst possible time. It can cause strife and division in the family and it can cost your family money if you don't take care of it now.

The Health Care Dilemma

Modern medical technology has made it much easier to recognize death but has made it harder to define it. We no longer have to invent ways to alert the living if we are accidentally buried alive. Yet, there are ways of being buried alive that do not involve coffins and earth. Terrible spiritual and legal struggles can take place if we do not clearly and legally define what measures are to be taken in a life-crisis and give someone clear legal authority and guidance to make decisions for us when we cannot do so ourselves. The toll on families can be enormous. Stress and legal costs can destroy a family, and in extreme cases, the media feeding frenzy is simply cruelty piled upon tragedy.

We must understand that the goal for all health care workers is saving life. We applaud their heroic efforts and dedication. The only death recognized by law, and therefore by health care facilities, is total brainstem death. By this definition, many patients can be forced to exist in a mechanized form of "living" burial. The health care maze of technological, legal, ethical, and economic gray areas makes it essential to be prepared for the many complexities of modern death.

Any patient who wants to have a say in his or her own care must express these wishes in detail. In order for written requests to be honored, however, any forms used must include a HIPAA release of liability for the doctors. Without a release of liability doctors simply will not allow one to die. Also, doctors and loved ones must know where the forms are. They should be on file with the physician, loved ones, the church and any healthcare facility the patient enters.

As Christians attempting to redeem our ancient traditions, we believe it is vital that the church family become the locus for preparation and storage of these papers. The clergy must take the lead in encouraging the education of their people not only in spiritual preparation but in this temporal preparation as well. The documents needed are readily available from most state governments, over the internet, through the mail or from a local attorney. Note that these forms, their contents and the requirements for each can vary from state to state.

If you have an attorney in the parish, help him or her hold a workshop discussing the need for the proper documents, and help parishioners prepare them. If you do not have an attorney in your parish, ask a local attorney.

The clergy must not only support, but lead this effort. Many times a pastor is forced into a difficult position by a tragic, unexpected death, for which the person was completely unprepared, with no documents at all. In such a case, the pastor often must become not only spiritual counselor and comforter, but organizer, negotiator, shopper and phone operator as well.

Necessary Documents

The essential documents to have are a Durable Power of Attorney, Living Will, Durable Health Care Power of Attorney, a Do Not Resuscitate order (DNR) if appropriate, and finally a Last Will and Testament. The Will is listed last because it becomes important only after the pronouncement of death.

CAUTION: The Durable Power of Attorney (DPOA) gives a person we name the right and ability to handle our legal and financial affairs at any time regardless of health or mental condition. Therefore the DPOA must be approached very carefully to guard against its being put into effect at any time for the wrong reasons. The person granted Power of Attorney must be totally trustworthy and the DPOA must be revisited should your life situation change due to divorce or death, etc. However, a serious injury, accident or illness can happen at any time. This could be for a term of years and can happen at any age. A DPOA is absolutely essential if you are about to begin caregiving for an elderly parent or terminally ill patient. If so, get this taken care of before the patient loses the legal ability to sign the document.

Personally, we are joint owners on all of our accounts, mortgages, cars, etc. We are each named beneficiaries on each other's insurance policies. However, much of our cash is in IRAS and Mark's 401-K. In the event Mark is incapacitated but still alive, life insurance policies will be of little help. The other funds may be needed for his care or survival of the household. Therefore, Mark has executed a DPOA naming Elizabeth. After forty years together we think it is a pretty safe thing to do. You must judge your own situation very carefully.

The Advance Directive for Healthcare (Living Will) stipulates what measures, if any, you wish to be taken to prolong your vital functions. You can define what measures should be taken, from "None" to "Every Heroic Measure." The Durable Health Care Power of Attorney (DHCPOA) appoints a person of your choice, and an alternate, to make life and death decisions on your behalf as you direct them in the Living Will.

A Do Not Resuscitate order (DNR) is usually reserved for the terminally ill, though some otherwise healthy adults also choose to have one. The term, "terminally ill" normally means that one has six months or less to live. Resuscitation carries numerous risks to the patient and can leave one, again, "living" a machine-driven life. The DNR should be on file with any facility the patient enters, clearly posted near their bed and on an arm bracelet. DNRs are routinely ignored as the health care workers' default position is, again, "every heroic measure" to save life. Some patients have been resuscitated only to live a machine-driven life for ten years or more. One terminal cancer patient had "DNR" tattooed on her chest.

One of the first steps your funeral society should take is to become familiar with your state laws and local legal protocols. Start by contacting your local hospital and coroner.

Generally, if an elderly parent dies at home, don't panic. Call 911, their physician and your pastor. Explain to the 911 operator that the death was expected and there is no emergency. Paramedics and police will arrive to pronounce death and do an initial investigation. Having their physician or hospice present, your pastor, and all your documents, including a proper DNR, can make this as painless as possible under the circumstances. If the patient is under hospice care they will take care of everything and 911 will not be necessary. The doctor can fill out the death certificate, and preparation for burial can begin immediately. If one desires a home and church funeral, there is no need to remove the body. In our county, only in the event of suspicious circumstances will the coroner come out to do a full investigation.

In the event of an accident around the home, etc., *Do Not Move The Body*. In the event of a tragic accident, where the victim has clearly been dead for some period of time, call 911 and explain the situation as calmly as possible. Paramedics will come and pronounce death. The police and coroner will investigate and will probably remove the body.

These are some of the instances where the other two documents we recommend will be helpful. Our coroner routinely works closely with religious representatives to avoid an autopsy unless absolutely necessary. A document describing the deceased's strong religious desire not to have an autopsy may be helpful.

These documents are not available from the usual legal and government sources. Some time ago the Orthodox Church in America (OCA) approached us to create a set of estate planning forms for Orthodox Christians that would be user-friendly, non-threatening and valid in all fifty states in the United States. Beginning with the forms that were included in the first edition of *A Christian Ending*, after numerous versions reviewed by attorneys, ethicists and the Synod of Bishops of the OCA, we have a very good final product. We're pleased to be able to show you these forms in Appendix B.

You can review them here but you can download them full size from the Orthodox Church in America website www.oca.org. Just search for *A Gift for My Loved Ones* and *Another Gift for My Loved Ones*. The first package includes all your essential estate planning forms and the second one has all your funeral planning information.

Since the first edition of *A Christian Ending* many States have created their own forms for funeral care often called Advance Directive for Funeral Care (ADFC). You can search your State's website to see if you have one. If not, our ADFC should serve you well. While they are not the typical documents that health care facilities are familiar with, they carry the same weight when they are signed and notarized. They are as much an indication of a person's final wishes as a Last Will and Testament.

The first document in *Another Gift for My Loved Ones* is an Advance Directive for Funeral Care or Death Care Power of Attorney. This document names an executor of your choice, and an alternate, to make all decisions relating to the care of your bodily remains. It also specifically prohibits any facility, hospital, or doctor from making any provisions or arrangements for your care, such as calling a funeral home or performing an autopsy.

The second form is your Pre-arranged Burial and Funeral Instructions. This form provides the person named in the Post Mortem Preference Document the vital information they will need to carry out your directives. The first document, just like the Living Will, DHCPOA, and DNR should be on file at any facility that you enter. It should also be distributed, along with the second document, to family and friends, especially the named executor of your Will, and should be on file in the church for the pastor or burial society to use.

Hospital morgues and coroners often have pre-arrangements with particular funeral homes to transport bodies. If you have an established funeral society in your church this is a completely unnecessary expense. Having a signed and notarized document expressly forbidding this will be helpful.

Funeral homes charge a fee for transporting to the funeral home. They also charge a fee for transferring the body to your preferred provider, who will also charge a receiving fee; a triple whammy. Each may also charge the basic services fee in addition.

In most states, a family member, agent holding a Durable Health Care Power of Attorney (DHCPOA) or other certified legal document (in our case the Advance Directive for Funeral Care) can act in lieu of a funeral director; fill out and file end-of-life documents; obtain a proper transport certificate and transport the deceased in any type of vehicle to any destination (funeral home, church, cemetery).

Some parishioners may want a spouse or family member to hold the DHCPOA but not have the burden of responsibility for the post mortem arrangements. Their named representative will have the power to delegate the preparation duties to the church community as needed. Copies of all these documents should be on file in the church office for safekeeping and emergency use. Don't forget to update the documents as names and circumstances change.

The last two sections of the Pre-arranged Burial and Funeral Instructions are personal and confidential. The obituary will not be needed immediately, and the Important Documents form is confidential. These should *not* be stored in the church office but in a safe place at home, where they can be easily found along with your Last Will and Testament. Do not store these important papers in your safe deposit box at the bank. Bank deposit boxes are sealed at the time of death and your important burial arrangement documents will not be accessible.

Necessary Documents:
Durable Power of Attorney
Advance Directive for Healthcare—Living Will
Durable Health Care Power of Attorney
Do Not Resuscitate order (DNR) as appropriate
Advance Directive for Funeral Care
 Death Care Power of Attorney
 Burial and Funeral Care Instructions
 Obituary information sheet (optional)
 Location of Important Documents (optional)
Last Will and Testament

There are numerous places you can go to find information on planning the funeral with the involvement of a mortuary funeral director. If you choose this method, do your homework ahead of time. Even summarizing the potential pitfalls here would take far too much space. It is never a good idea to pre-pay a funeral director for your funeral. If your church family handles everything it won't cost much anyway.

13.

Pre-Planning in Community

Aim at heaven and you get earth thrown in.
Aim at earth and you get neither.
— C. S. LEWIS

When the power of love overcomes the
love of power the world will know peace.
— JIMI HENDRIX

UNFORTUNATELY PEOPLE OFTEN have to plan a funeral during a time of intense emotional pain and shock. In a thriving church community, this should not be the case. The clergy must be willing to discuss this subject openly with the whole church. If there is no education before the crisis, what chance is there that we will know how to handle the crisis when it arrives? The death of a loved one or a member of the community is inevitable. If we plan and work together at least as well as we do on our favorite annual fund-raiser, the burden on the family will be greatly reduced and the community will reap rewards far greater than those of a fund-raiser.

As Christians we live in community, and we certainly should die in community. We are one body. We partake of the one cup. A death in the family should be a family event. There are individual preparations which must be made, primarily for legal purposes. There are also community preparations that should be made so that the whole community plays a role in the preparation and burial of our brethren.

Something for Everyone

There are many roles to play, from making phone calls and hotel reservations to hands-on preparation of the corpse for burial. Each member has his or her own gifts to offer for this service. There is so much to do that there is something for everyone, including the children. Every small deed taken on by the church family is one less burden or expense for the bereaved family.

Each person should do no more than they are capable of. Yet each of us should approach these tasks courageously, as Saint John Chrysostom teaches. In the face of death, we Christians stretch ourselves beyond the limits of our neo-pagan societal norms. As we serve others, the Lord leads and gives us strength to do things we never thought we could.

It is important that the bereaved family not be left to make all of the arrangements of the "customary" American funeral on their own. The pitfalls of such an endeavor are far too numerous for those without the training or the emotional stamina. Nor can the pastor be expected to serve the family's spiritual needs and also make the arrangements. At the very least, the pastor needs to identify those people who are willing to help in the time of greatest need. A couple of people who are willing to guide and support the bereaved family through the arrangements, negotiate fees and make sure they are not taken advantage of will be a great blessing.

At best, we should establish formal burial societies, such as those known in Byzantium, to take over any duties specified by the deceased that the family wishes to relinquish. Each situation is different and some families will want to be closely involved, while others may not. All will greatly appreciate the love, honor and care shown by the community.

Haste Makes Waste

Take your time and be thorough in your decision-making if you find yourself dealing with the funeral industry. It is important to have a working knowledge of what you are getting into. First you must know your state's funeral laws. Most states have their entire code of laws online now and it's very easy to find what you're looking for. You must read all the statutes and the regulations promulgated by the regulatory agency. You'll be surprised how little funeral law there is in most states. Remember too that most of the regulations apply to "professional" funeral directors, not to families and churches. You'll learn to recognize the difference. Mark read every funeral statute and regulation for the State of South Carolina. After reading all of that, the last line said, "these regulations do not apply to private family and church funerals." There are literally no laws regulating church and family funerals in our state.

This knowledge will come in handy when dealing with funeral directors. They seem to love to quote the law to us whether they know the law or not.

Our small community has researched the local funeral home price lists as well as cemeteries and monument companies. This information can be handy in a crisis. Some of the books listed in our bibliography are a good source of basic knowledge regarding the funeral industry.

Every thriving Christian community should have a small group of people dedicated to visitation. Visitation of the sick, elderly and shut-ins need not be left to the clergy alone. This group can quickly become the nucleus for a burial society. These visitation volunteers can help keep the pastor and congregation informed of the health of those they visit.

Healthcare professionals are generally quite used to moving and cleaning bodies. They are often more than willing to participate in the preparation team as an extension of their professional care.

Fortunately, funerals are not daily events. We hope they will be very few and very far between. Our small church hasn't had a funeral in nearly three years. We interviewed the priest in one of the largest Orthodox churches in the United States. His church averages about one funeral per month. This is all the more reason to organize and compartmentalize the community's involvement. A church this size could have more than one preparation and transportation team. Using their particular gifts and talents, each member can specialize in different areas of need.

Organization

One thing should be very clear: death in the church family is not a casual affair. It should be taken very seriously by all the members so that each will be ready to participate. It may require sacrifices such as taking some vacation time off from work.

Because of the ebb and flow of natural human biorhythms, physical life-sustaining activity is at its lowest ebb at night. Consequently, most natural deaths occur at around 3 AM. Those who volunteer for the preparation and burial society must know this from the beginning. Volunteers should feel honored to receive that most infrequent late night call to come to the aid of a member in need.

Assemble a kit for preparation of the body (Appendix A). One can be kept in a readily accessible location at the church. We use an old airline carry-on suitcase from the thrift store to hold everything needed. It is always packed and ready.

Organization is as individual as the community. You may have several fully prepared teams or your entire effort may be just three people. Only you can determine what is best for your community.

There are numerous duties and arrangements to be made besides the hands-on preparation of the body for burial. Volunteers are needed for as many as your community can handle. Funeral directors will be happy to provide some of the others for a fee.

1. **Visiting the sick.** We strongly believe that any funeral ministry should start with a visitation ministry. Some people just naturally visit anyone who is sick or in the hospital, others don't but would be happy to if they were part of a supporting ministry. This group can be a great help in keeping the pastor informed as well as a delight to the people they visit.

2. **Prayer and notification.** These volunteers are available to help the pastor before and at the time of death. Disabled or home-bound volunteers can help with prayer from home and notification needs by phone. Others pray, chant hymns or read the Psalter on-site. They

can also be prepared to help the family, bring coffee, clean up, prepare food, etc., as needed, or stay out of the way, as the case may be. This group keeps the preparation and the transportation teams informed and prepared for an expected death.

3. **Funeral home liaison.** Do your homework and be familiar with the industry and the local funeral homes.

4. **Preparation team.** The preparation team comes in just before or after the death, when called by the visitation team. This team performs the actual preparation of the body for burial as described in chapters 8 and 9. Remember, it only takes two people; three with a reader. You may want to have a men's and a women's team; this is beautiful but it is not necessary. Each team should have three or four members with alternates to cover for vacations, illness, etc. Since they have been kept informed, they will be prepared and ready for the call.

5. **Dry ice.** Obtain two days' dry ice for the preparation team (30 lbs. cut in three 2 in. and two 1 in. sheets). This can be done the next day. The body will be just fine at room temperature for 24—36 hours. Pelletized dry ice can also be used.

6. **Transportation team.** The transportation team transports the coffin to the home or facility. They assist in placing the deceased in the coffin and then transport the body to the church for the Vigil. Obviously, there is lifting involved here so they need to be prepared for it.

7. **Travel across state lines.** There are no federal laws prohibiting or controlling the transportation of a corpse across state lines. It is perfectly legal, with the proper transport certificate, to load grandma up in the van or pickup and drive her back to the old homestead yourself. It may be somewhat unreasonable to ask the church burial society to do it, however. Commercial carriers have their own requirements which you will need to be aware of. Funeral directors will try to tell you they cannot ship a body by air if it is not embalmed. This is not true. We have done it. It can get complicated at the destination because the people there are accustomed to dealing with funeral directors. Sometimes it is just easier to pay the professionals for this service.

8. **Building the casket or coffin.** Any competent weekend woodworker can build a perfectly good, even beautiful casket or coffin for use by the church. Our community has one available at all times for emergencies. There are several good Orthodox coffin makers listed by region on our website, achristianending.com. Some of them ship anywhere in the United States overnight.

   Many retail casket outlets have sprung up including discounters such as CostCo. There is also the possibility of renting a casket used for viewings before cremation. The inner cardboard cremation container can then be used for transportation and burial. This is perfectly acceptable and not at all disrespectful. The cost is around $25. No coffin at all is also perfectly acceptable and dignified. Mark would prefer to be wrapped in a shroud rather than placed in a box. There are several internet casket sites that offer free shipping or overnight shipping for a fee. The least expensive acceptable casket is usually called a Jewish casket. Several custom casket makers can ship overnight anywhere in the United States.

9. **Filing the paperwork** (Death Certificate/Vital Records form, Transport and Final Disposition of Remains certificates, and any other legal forms). At least one volunteer should be familiar with all the local requirements. They must know how and where to obtain forms and where to file them. An attorney, hospice or the County Coroner may be able to help explain local procedures.

10. **Family and friends notification** (phone calls). Your church probably already has a phone tree and/or email list for notifying parishioners of important events. These volunteers use the "Contact" list provided on the Pre-arrangement form. They should also have another form to record answers to certain questions. Will they be traveling? Will they need accommodations? Will they need a ride from the airport/train station/bus station? When will they arrive? Then the volunteers will coordinate with the shuttle service team.

11. **Answer the phone for the family.** Graciously explain that the family is grieving and give available details of arrangements. Keep a phone log for the family, for future reference and for returning calls.

12. **Write and place the obituary.**
13. **Arrange for flowers.** Some people have a flair for arranging flowers. Doing the arrangements in-house can save the family money.
14. **Prepare the church.**
15. **Cemetery liaison.** Do your homework and watch for pitfalls. The ideal is for the body to be in contact with the earth. Liners are acceptable. Never use a vault. Vaults were created to contain embalming fluid leaking from bodies. There is absolutely no good reason for a natural burial to require a vault. If the cemetery requires one it should have drain holes and be filled with earth.

    Commercial cemeteries are for-profit businesses on private property. They have the right to require whatever they wish on their property. Likewise, you have the right to go elsewhere.
16. **Dig the grave** if in a private cemetery.
17. **Arrange for a marker or monument.** Do your homework and watch for pitfalls such as double billing by the cemetery and the monument company. Some cemeteries charge an extra fee for using an outside monument company.
18. **Obtain a guest book.** (The church should have an extra one.)
19. **Make hotel reservations** or other arrangements for family.
20. **Set up airport or train shuttle service.**
21. **Prepare food** or arrange catering or restaurant reservations.
22. **Readers.** Last, but most certainly not least, organize a team of readers.

Perhaps the most challenging and forgotten part of the traditional ancient Christian funeral is the reading of the Psalter. Ideally, the deceased should not be left alone and the Psalter should be read without stop from the time of death to the beginning of the funeral service. This includes the time of the visitation except during a Panikhida or Trisagion Prayers. Family members should be encouraged to take part. The important thing is that constant prayer and vigil is maintained for the deceased. We all need all the prayers we can get at this, or any other time.

Some may find it eerie to be alone in the church at night with a dead body. It is important that members stay within their comfort level. It is equally important to remember that all our fears regarding dead bodies, restless spirits and ghosts are based on paganism and superstition, much of it sold to us by Hollywood. We are called to be courageous and perform all these duties, even the most difficult ones, with love for the deceased. Love endures all things and conquers all. Readers may want to work in pairs.

If you've ever read by the tomb of Christ on Holy Friday night and Holy Saturday morning then you know how powerful the reading of the Psalms can be. If you haven't experienced it, we encourage you to give it a try.

Many of the listed duties do not require the same amount of dedication as the actual body preparation or vigil, but they are just as important. There is something for everyone.

Don't forget to follow up with the bereaved family over the coming days and months. Identify members in need of comfort and add them to the visitation list for additional attention. The ancient church prescribed that memorial services be performed at three days, nine days, forty days and annually from the date of repose. Modern psychology has confirmed that these periods mark particular milestones in the grieving process. It should be no surprise to the believer that science confirms what the church has known for millennia. It is important that the church family stay close to the bereaved family. A phone call or personal visit from the church family, not just the pastor, can do wonders for the bereaved, who may feel isolated and cut off in their grief.

It's Up to Us

If it has the will, the dedication, and the love to do so, any community can perform a complete funeral *at no cost* to the bereaved family. There are costs certainly. There are costs for flowers, candles, casket or other container, a monument and document filing fees. If possible, all of these costs should routinely be born by the church community. If the family is struggling, we have done a great service and have secured treasure in heaven. If the family is wealthy, we hope that the funds that would have been expended on a lavish "customary" funeral will be donated to the church building fund or to a worthy charity.

At our church, when someone dies we naturally assume that the church will take care of everything. This doesn't mean we must do it but that we are prepared to do it. There are many ways we can work with a professional to make sure the family gets what they want. We never discuss money. Yet, our church has been beautifully adorned by the most generous gifts of families we've helped through this process.

One of the most worthy causes is the cemetery acquisition fund. The final link in our ability to redeem the entire process of traditional ancient Christian burial is having our own consecrated land in which to bury our own people, facing east, in the simplest, most ecologically friendly way. We don't need much land. You can get 500 graves in one acre of land and we recycle.

Owning our own land could help revive another ancient tradition: the Ossuary, or Bone House. These are still found in many monasteries and some old-world cemeteries. After ten to twelve years in contact with the earth the human body is completely decomposed to bone. The bones are then dug up, cleaned and stored in a building made especially for this purpose. The grave is reused. This wonderful ancient tradition serves as a constant reminder that physical death is imminent for each of us and that the only true death is sin.

The effort to revive ancient burial traditions can reach across jurisdictional lines to become a truly Christian effort. Local churches should join forces and share resources in forming burial societies and purchasing cemetery property. It may not be reasonable to expect everyone from each church to attend every funeral (as wonderful as that might be). Surely the preparation, transportation and cemetery teams can coordinate and share resources. This would have many practical and financial advantages, not to mention the community spiritual growth that it would foster.

14.

A Service for the Preparation of the Dead for Burial

WHEN WE CONSIDERED the long history of Christian preparation of the dead, some details of which were even made law under Emperor Justinian, we were somewhat surprised not to find a rite or service pertaining specifically to this holy and momentous act of the Christian community. There certainly may be one. We just haven't found it.

It is perfectly acceptable and traditional to read the Psalter during the preparation of the body for burial, just as it is read continuously from death to the beginning of the funeral. You may have a recording ready if there is no reader present. This is also quite acceptable. The main thing is to maintain an attitude of simplicity, love and reverence during this time of preparation.

Even though there is no way of knowing what happens to the soul at the moment of death and shortly thereafter, we find in some of the ancient literature and from some anecdotal evidence that the soul of the departed may be nearby. Some writers also indicate that the soul may be disoriented and dismayed by its new state of being. We must also consider the bereaved family.

We encourage family members and friends to stay and pray, observe, read, or even help in the preparation of their loved one for burial. This is a very delicate time for the bereaved. For this reason, we have tried to select readings that reflect the love of God for the deceased and for all mankind. We endeavor to use Psalms and Scripture readings that emphasize this love, as well as our love and trust in the goodness of God. The time for lamentation will come during the vigil and the funeral itself. This time, though, is the very cusp of a new way of life for those who must live without their beloved. It is also the beginning of a new state of being for the deceased.

In these selected readings and prayers we try to offer comfort to the bereaved despite the busyness of the preparation. If in some unknown way our words may also offer some solace, focus or direction for the departed soul, so much the better. All Scripture reading is indeed very good and profitable for all souls. Giving some thought to the deceased and the bereaved while selecting these particular readings certainly can do no harm.

The readings are arranged much as they are in most Orthodox Christian services. We begin with the Trisagion Prayers and the prayer before beginning any task. There are two sections of twelve Psalms followed by an Old Testament reading, an Epistle reading and a Gospel reading, with a few hymns and prayers interspersed, followed by a closing prayer. These prayers and readings are appropriate to be done without the priest. The priest or pastor will want to be spending his time with the family and organizing the other activities that need to take place in preparation for the vigil and funeral.

There is enough material here to last approximately forty-five minutes to an hour. If you complete your work before the reading is complete, simply skip to the prayers at the conclusion of the preparation (p. 165). Should the team require more time than the readings allow, then simply begin the reading of the Psalms with Psalm 1, or repeat the Psalms and prayers contained here.

Any words that would require alteration depending on the sex of the deceased are given in the masculine but placed in italics as a reminder to make appropriate alteration. The letter *N.* refers to the name of the deceased.

We pray that this humble offering is acceptable and helpful to all.

When the initial preparations have been made, the icons are in place, the body is positioned and respectfully covered, those assembled shall stop their activities and pray.

The priest, if present, begins:
Blessed is our God, always, now and ever and unto ages of ages. Amen.

Otherwise a reader begins thus:
Through the prayers of our holy Fathers, O Lord Jesus Christ our God, have mercy upon us and save us. Amen.

Glory to thee, O God, glory to thee.

O heavenly King, the Comforter, the Spirit of Truth, who art everywhere and fillest all things, Treasury of blessings and Giver of life, come and abide in us, and cleanse us from every impurity, and save our souls, O Good One.*

Holy God, holy mighty, holy immortal: have mercy on us. (*thrice*)

Glory to the Father and to the Son and to the Holy Spirit, now and ever and unto ages of ages. Amen.

All-holy Trinity, have mercy on us. Lord, cleanse us from our sins. Master, pardon our transgressions. Holy One, visit and heal our infirmities for thy Name's sake.

Lord, have mercy. (*thrice*)

Glory to the Father and to the Son and to the Holy Spirit, now and ever and unto ages of ages. Amen.

Our Father, who art in heaven, hallowed be thy Name; thy kingdom come; thy will be done, on earth as it is in heaven. Give us this day our daily bread, and forgive us our trespasses as we forgive those who trespass against us; and lead us not into temptation, but deliver us from the evil one.

---

* *From Pascha to Pentecost* Glory to thee… *and* O heavenly King… *are omitted. From Pascha to Ascension they are replaced by* Christ is risen from the dead, trampling down death by death and upon those in the tombs bestowing life. (*thrice*)

Priest, if present: For thine is the kingdom and the power and the glory of the Father and of the Son and of the Holy Spirit, now and ever and unto ages of ages. Amen.

Or reader: Through the prayers of our holy Fathers, O Lord Jesus Christ our God, have mercy on us and save us. Amen.

If it is the time of a great feast its troparion may be sung here.

The Symbol of Faith

I believe in one God, the Father almighty, Maker of heaven and earth, and of all things visible and invisible;

and in one Lord Jesus Christ, the Son of God, the Only-begotten, begotten of the Father before all ages, Light of Light, true God of true God, begotten, not made, of one essence with the Father, by whom all things were made; who, for us men and for our salvation, came down from heaven, and was incarnate of the Holy Spirit and the Virgin Mary and became man, and was crucified also for us under Pontius Pilate, and suffered and was buried, and the third day he rose again, according to the Scriptures, and ascended into heaven, and sits at the right hand of the Father, and he shall come again with glory to judge the living and the dead; whose kingdom shall have no end;

and in the Holy Spirit, the Lord and Giver of Life, who proceeds from the Father, who with the Father and the Son together is worshipped and glorified, who spoke by the Prophets;

and in One, Holy, Catholic, and Apostolic Church. I acknowledge one Baptism for the remission of sins. I look for the Resurrection of the dead, and the life of the world to come. Amen.

Prayer Before Commencing

Priest or reader:

Almighty God, our help and refuge, fountain of wisdom and tower of strength, who knowest that we can do nothing without thy guidance and help; assist us, we pray thee, and direct us to divine wisdom and power, that we may accomplish this task of preparing the body of thy departed servant N. for burial, faithfully and diligently, according to thy will, so that it may be profitable to *him*, to ourselves and others, and to the glory of thy holy Name. For thine is the kingdom and the power and the glory of the Father, and of the Son and of the Holy Spirit, now and ever and unto ages of ages. Amen.

Beloved *brother* in Christ N., forgive us.

Now we begin the preparation of the body.

If there is no deacon or priest, a reader or layman may read the Gospel lessons. If the preparation of the body is completed before the conclusion of the readings, read to the end of the current psalm, scripture or prayer, and then skip to the concluding prayers on page 165.

Reader: Come, let us worship God our King.

Come, let us worship and fall down before Christ our King and our God.

Come, let us worship and fall down before Christ himself, our King and our God.

PSALM 3

Lord, why do they that afflict me keep multiplying? Many are they that rise up against me. Many are they who say to my soul: There is no salvation for him in his God. But thou, O Lord, art my protector, my glory and the one who lifts up my head. I cried to the Lord with my voice and he heard me from his holy hill. I lay down and slept; I awoke, for the Lord will protect me. I will not be afraid of ten thousands of people who set themselves against me all around. Arise, O Lord, save me, O my God, for thou hast struck all those who are my enemies without cause, thou hast broken the teeth of the sinners. Salvation is from the Lord and thy blessing is upon thy people.

PSALM 8

O Lord, our Lord, how wondrous is thy name in all the earth, for thy splendor is exalted far beyond the heavens. From the mouths of babes and nursing infants thou hast brought forth perfect praise because of thine enemies that thou mayest silence enemy and avenger. For I shall look at the heavens, the works of thy fingers, the moon and stars that thou hast established. What is man that thou rememberest him, or the son of man that thou comest to him? For thou hast made him a little lower than the angels and thou hast crowned him with glory and honor. Thou hast made him to rule over the works of thy hands, thou hast put all things under his feet, all sheep and oxen—even the beasts of the field, the birds of the heavens and the fish of the sea and all things passing through the paths of the sea. O Lord, our Lord, how wondrous is thy name in all the earth.

PSALM 16

Hear me, O Lord of my righteousness, attend to my supplication, give ear to my prayer free from deceit. From thy countenance let my vindication come, let my eyes behold uprightness. Thou hast tested my heart, visiting in the night, thou hast tried me and found nothing unjust. To keep my mouth from the talk of men's deeds, through the words of thy lips I held to hard ways. Restore my steps in thy paths that my footsteps may not slip. I have called upon thee, for thou hast listened, O God, incline thine ear to me and hear my speech. Show forth thy wondrous mercy, saving them that hope in thee from those who rise against thy right hand. Keep me as the apple of thine eye; in the shelter of thy wings thou wilt shelter me from the unholy faces afflicting me, from the deadly enemies surrounding my soul. They are enclosed in their own fat, with their mouth they speak proudly. Casting me out, they have now surrounded me, inclining their eyes down to the earth, like a lion ready to tear its prey, like a young lion lurking in secret places. Arise, O Lord, outrun them, cast them down, deliver my soul from the wicked, thy sword from the enemies of thy hand. Lord, separate thy few from the earth, even in their lifetimes. And those whose belly was filled with thy treasures, like their swine, were satisfied and left the remnants to their children. As for me, in righteousness I shall behold thy countenance, I shall be satisfied in beholding thy glory.

PSALM 18

The heavens declare the glory of God, the firmament shows the works of his hands. Day unto day utters speech and night unto night reveals knowledge. There is no speech nor language where their voice is not heard. Their voice has gone out through all the earth, their words to the ends of the world. He has set his tabernacle in the sun, which comes forth like a bridegroom from the bridal chamber, exulting like a strong man set to run the course. Its rising is from one end of heaven, its circuit running to the other; nothing can hide from the heat of it. The law of the Lord is perfect, converting the soul, the testimony of the Lord is sure, making children wise, the statutes of the Lord are right, rejoicing the heart, the commandment of the Lord is pure, enlightening the eyes, the fear of the Lord is clean, enduring forever, the judgments of the Lord are true and righteous altogether. More to be desired are they than gold and precious stones, sweeter also than honey and the honeycomb. For indeed thy servant keeps them, in keeping them there is great reward. Who can understand his own transgressions? Cleanse me from secret faults, and from those of others spare thy servant. If they have no dominion over me, then I shall be blameless and I shall be cleansed of great transgression. The words of my mouth and my heart's meditation will be continually pleasing in thy presence, O Lord, my strength and my redeemer.

PSALM 21

O God, my God, hear me: why hast thou forsaken me? So far from saving me are my roaring words. O my God, all day I cry out to thee and thou dost not hear me, all night, and I do no wrong in this. Thou dwellest in the sanctuary, O praise of Israel. Our fathers hoped in thee, they hoped in thee and thou didst deliver them. They cried to thee and they were saved, they hoped in thee and were not disgraced. But I am a worm, and no man, a reproach of men and despised by the people. All those who see me ridicule me, their lips babbling, their heads wagging: he hoped in the Lord, let him rescue him, let him save him since he delights in him. For thou art he that drew me out from the womb, my hope from my mother's breast, I was cast upon thee from the womb, from my mother's womb thou art my God. Do not stand off from me, for affliction is near and there is no one to help. Many young bulls have surrounded me, fat bulls have encircled me. They open wide their mouths against me, like a raging and roaring lion. I am poured out like water, my bones are all scattered, my heart is like wax melting into my stomach. My strength is dried up like a potsherd, my tongue cleaves to my throat; thou hast led me into the dust of death. For many dogs have surrounded me, a mob of evildoers has enclosed me, they have pierced my hands and my feet. They number all my bones, they look and stare at me. They divide my garments among them, and for my clothing they cast lots. But, O Lord, do not take thy help from me, attend to my aid. Free my soul from the sword, my only-begotten from the dog's hand; save me from the lion's mouth, my humility from the ox's horns. I will declare thy name to my brethren, amidst the assembly I will sing to thee. You who fear the Lord, praise him, all you descendants of Jacob, glorify him, and fear him, all you offspring of Israel. For he has not despised nor scorned the beggar's plea, nor has he hid his face from me, and when I cried to him, he heard. My praise is from thee in the great assembly, I will pay my vows before them that fear thee. The poor shall eat and be satisfied, those who seek him will praise the Lord, their hearts will live forever. All the ends of the world shall remember and turn to the Lord, and all families of the nations shall worship before thee, for the kingdom is the Lord's, and he rules over the nations. All the prosperous of the earth have eaten and worshiped; all those going down into the earth shall bow down before him. My soul lives on in him. And my seed shall serve him, the coming generation shall be told of the Lord and they will declare his righteousness to a people who will be born, whom the Lord has made.

PSALM 22

The Lord is my shepherd, I shall not want. In green pastures he makes me a home, he nourishes me beside the still water. He uplifts my soul, he leads me in the paths of righteousness for his name's sake. Though

I walk in the shadow of death, I will fear no evil, for thou art with me, thy rod and thy staff, they comfort me. Thou preparest me a table in my persecutors' presence, thou anointest my head with oil, and the cup thou givest me to drink—how supremely good it is! And thy mercy shall pursue me all the days of my life, and I shall dwell in the Lord's house for the length of my days.

PSALM 56

Have mercy on me, O God, have mercy, for my soul trusts always in thee; and in the shadow of thy wings I will hope until iniquity shall pass away. I will cry out to God Most High, my God who is my benefactor. He has sent out from heaven and saved me, he gave over to reproach those trampling me down. God has sent out his mercy and his truth and delivered my soul from young lions. I lay down like one troubled, amid sons of men, their teeth spears and arrows, their tongue a sharp sword. Be exalted, O God, above the heavens; let thy glory be above all the earth. They have set a snare for my steps, they bowed down my soul, they dug a pit right before me but fell into it themselves. My heart is ready, O God, my heart is ready, I will sing and give praise in my glory. Awake, my glory, awake, lute and harp! I will arise at daybreak. I will praise thee, O Lord, among the peoples, I will sing to thee among the nations. For thy mercy is magnified to the heavens, thy truth even to the clouds. Be exalted, O God, above the heavens, let thy glory be above all the earth.

PSALM 62

O God, my God, at dawn I seek thee, my soul thirsted for thee, my flesh so many times has thirsted for thee in a trackless desert where no water is. So in the sanctuary I have appeared before thee to see thy power and thy glory. Because thy mercy is better than life, my lips shall sing praise to thee. Thus I will bless thee in my life, I will lift up my hands in thy name. As if with marrow and fatness, my soul was made full, and my mouth shall sing praise to thee with lips filled with rejoicing. When I remembered thee on my bed at daybreak I meditated on thee.

For thou art become my helper, and in the shelter of thy wings I will be glad and rejoice. My soul has cleaved to thee, thy right hand has upheld me. But those who sought vainly my soul shall go into the lowest places of earth. They shall be given the sword's edge, they shall be portion for foxes. But the king shall rejoice in God, all who swear by him shall be praised, for the mouths of liars are stopped.

PSALM 70

In thee, O Lord, I have hoped, may I never be put to shame. Deliver me in thy righteousness, rescue me, incline thine ear to me and save me. Be the God of my protection, the stronghold of my salvation, for thou art my rock and my refuge. O my God, rescue me from the sinner's hand, from his transgressing and cruel hands. For thou art my endurance, O Lord, my hope, O Lord, from my youth. By thee I have been upheld from birth, from my mother's womb thou hast been my shelter, my song shall be always of thee. I have become as a wonder to many, but thou art my strong helper. Let my mouth be filled with thy praise that I may sing of thy glory, sing thy magnificence all the day. Do not cast me off in the time of old age, when my strength fails do not forsake me. For my enemies spoke against me, those stalking my soul have conspired against me, saying: God has abandoned him, pursue and lay hold of him, for there is none to rescue him. O God, stand not far off from me; my God, make haste for my help. Let those slandering my soul be disgraced and vanish away, let those seeking my hurt be covered in shame and reproach. But I will hope continually and will praise thee yet more and more. My mouth shall proclaim thy righteousness, thy salvation all the day long, for I know nothing about the worldly business of men. I shall enter into the Lord's power, I shall remember, O Lord, thy righteousness, thine only. Thou hast taught me, O God, from my youth, and from then until now I will proclaim thy wonders. Even to my old age and great years, O God, do not abandon me, until I proclaim thy strength to all the coming generations, thy power and thy righteousness. O God, the magnificent things thou hast done for me reach even to the very heights—O God, who is like thee? How great and severe the afflictions thou hast shown me, yet thou didst relent and quicken me, thou hast led me up from the great depths of earth. Thou didst increase thy greatness over me, then thou didst turn and comfort me, thou hast led me up from the great depths of earth. I shall sing thy truth, O God, in the vessel of a psalm, I shall sing praise with the harp, O Holy One of Israel. My lips shall greatly rejoice when I sing praises to thee, and so shall my soul rejoice which thou hast redeemed. My tongue shall study thy righteousness all the day long whenever those seeking my hurt are disgraced and confounded.

PSALM 83

How beloved thy dwellings, O Lord of hosts. My soul longs, even faints for the courts of the Lord, my heart and my flesh have rejoiced in the living God. For the sparrow has found a home, the turtledove a nest for herself where she will lay her young—even thine altars, O Lord of hosts, my King and my God. Blessed are those who dwell in thy house, they shall praise thee unto ages of ages. Blessed is the man, O Lord, whose help comes from thee, whose heart has ascended into the high valley of weeping, into the place thou hast set, for the lawgiver shall bestow blessings. They shall go from strength to strength, the God of gods shall be seen appearing in Zion. O Lord God of hosts, hear my prayer, give ear, O God of Jacob! O God, our protector, behold: look upon the face of thy Christ. For one day in thy courts is better than a thousand elsewhere, I would rather be laid low in the house of my God than dwell in the tents of the wicked. For the Lord loves mercy and truth, God will bestow grace and glory, the Lord will never deny good things to those who walk in innocence. O Lord of hosts, blessed is the man who sets his hope in thee.

PSALM 102

Bless the Lord, O my soul, all that is within me, bless his holy name. Bless the Lord, O my soul, and forget not all he has given, who forgives all thine iniquities, who heals all thy diseases, who redeems thy life from corruption, who crowns thee with mercy and compassion, who satisfies thy desire with good things, and thy youth is renewed like the eagle's. The Lord performs great works of mercy and justice for all the oppressed. He made known his ways to Moses, and his will to Israel's sons. The Lord is merciful and gracious, slow to anger and abounding in mercy. He will never be fully enraged, nor will he keep his anger forever. He did not deal our sins back to us, nor give us what our evils deserved. As far as heaven extends over earth, so the Lord has made his mercy extend over those who fear him. As far as the east stands from the west, so far has he taken our sins from us. As a father has compassion for sons, so will the Lord have compassion upon those who fear him, for he well knows our fashioning, he has remembered that we are dust. As for man, his days are like grass, as a flower of the field so he flourishes. Then the wind has passed over and he shall be gone, he shall no longer know the place. But the Lord's mercy is for all eternity upon all those who fear him, and his righteousness upon sons of sons, to such as shall keep his covenant and remember to do his commandments. The Lord prepared his throne in heaven, his kingship is supreme over all. Bless the Lord, all you his angels, mighty in strength to do his word, in hearing the sound of his words. Bless the Lord, all you his hosts, his ministers that obey his will. Bless the Lord, all his works, in all places of his dominion. Bless the Lord, O my soul.

PSALM 114

I am filled with love, for the Lord shall hearken to the voice of my supplication, for he inclined his ear to me, and throughout all my days I shall call out to him. The agonies of death surrounded me, the dangers of hell loomed over me, I found affliction and grief. Then I called upon the Lord's name: O Lord, deliver my soul. The Lord is merciful and righteous, and God has mercy on us. The Lord is the guardian of infants; I was brought low and he saved me. Return, O my soul, to your peace, the Lord has been very good to you, he has delivered my soul from death, my eyes from tears, and my feet from faltering. I shall be well-pleasing to the Lord in the land of the living.

Glory to the Father and to the Son and to the Holy Spirit, now and ever and unto ages of ages. Amen.

Alleluia. Alleluia. Alleluia. Glory to thee, O God. (*thrice*)

Lord, have mercy. (*thrice*)

Troparion for the Departed

TONE FOUR

With the spirits of the righteous departed, give rest, O Savior, to the soul of thy servant, preserving *him* in the blessed life which is with thee, who lovest mankind.

In the place of thy rest, O Lord, where all thy saints repose, give rest also to the soul of thy servant, for thou alone lovest mankind.

Glory to the Father and to the Son and to the Holy Spirit.

Thou art the God who descended into hell and loosed the bonds of the captives. Give rest also to the soul of thy servant.

Now and ever and unto ages of ages. Amen.

O Virgin, alone pure and blameless, who didst bear God without seed, intercede that the soul of thy servant may be saved.

Reader: The reading from the book of Genesis. (1:1–2:15)

In the beginning God created the heavens and the earth. The earth was without form and void, and darkness was upon the face of the deep; and the Spirit of God was moving over the face of the waters.

And God said, "Let there be light"; and there was light. And God saw that the light was good; and God separated the light from the darkness. God called the light Day, and the darkness he called Night. And there was evening and there was morning, one day.

And God said, "Let there be a firmament in the midst of the waters, and let it separate the waters from the waters." And God made the firmament and separated the waters which were under the firmament from the waters which were above the firmament. And it was so. And God called the firmament heaven. And there was evening and there was morning, a second day.

And God said, "Let the waters under the heavens be gathered

together into one place, and let the dry land appear." And it was so. God called the dry land Earth, and the waters that were gathered together he called Seas. And God saw that it was good. And God said, "Let the earth put forth vegetation, plants yielding seed, and fruit trees bearing fruit in which is their seed, each according to its kind, upon the earth." And it was so. The earth brought forth vegetation, plants yielding seed according to their own kinds, and trees bearing fruit in which is their seed, each according to its kind. And God saw that it was good. And there was evening and there was morning, a third day.

And God said, "Let there be lights in the firmament of the heavens to separate the day from the night; and let them be for signs and for seasons and for days and years, and let them be lights in the firmament of the heavens to give light upon the earth." And it was so. And God made the two great lights, the greater light to rule the day, and the lesser light to rule the night; he made the stars also. And God set them in the firmament of the heavens to give light upon the earth, to rule over the day and over the night, and to separate the light from the darkness. And God saw that it was good. And there was evening and there was morning, a fourth day.

And God said, "Let the waters bring forth swarms of living creatures, and let birds fly above the earth across the firmament of the heavens." So God created the great sea monsters and every living creature that moves, with which the waters swarm, according to their kinds, and every winged bird according to its kind. And God saw that it was good. And God blessed them, saying, "Be fruitful and multiply and fill the waters in the seas, and let birds multiply on the earth." And there was evening and there was morning, a fifth day.

And God said, "Let the earth bring forth living creatures according to their kinds: cattle and creeping things and beasts of the earth according to their kinds." And it was so. And God made the beasts of the earth according to their kinds and the cattle according to their kinds, and everything that creeps upon the ground according to its kind. And God saw that it was good.

Then God said, "Let us make man in our image, after our likeness;

and let them have dominion over the fish of the sea, and over the birds of the air, and over the cattle, and over all the earth, and over every creeping thing that creeps upon the earth." So God created man in his own image, in the image of God he created him; male and female he created them. And God blessed them, and God said to them, "Be fruitful and multiply, and fill the earth and subdue it; and have dominion over the fish of the sea and over the birds of the air and over every living thing that moves upon the earth."

And God said, "Behold, I have given you every plant yielding seed which is upon the face of all the earth, and every tree with seed in its fruit; you shall have them for food. And to every beast of the earth, and to every bird of the air, and to everything that creeps on the earth, everything that has the breath of life, I have given every green plant for food." And it was so.

And God saw everything that he had made, and behold, it was very good. And there was evening and there was morning, a sixth day.

Thus the heavens and the earth were finished, and all the host of them. And on the seventh day God finished his work which he had done, and he rested on the seventh day from all his work which he had done. So God blessed the seventh day and hallowed it, because on it God rested from all his work which he had done in creation.

These are the generations of the heavens and the earth when they were created. In the day that the Lord God made the earth and the heavens, when no plant of the field was yet in the earth and no herb of the field had yet sprung up—for the Lord God had not caused it to rain upon the earth, and there was no man to till the ground; but a mist went up from the earth and watered the whole face of the ground— then the Lord God formed man of dust from the ground, and breathed into his nostrils the breath of life; and man became a living being.

And the Lord God planted a garden in Eden, in the east; and there he put the man whom he had formed. And out of the ground the Lord God made to grow every tree that is pleasant to the sight and good for food, the tree of life also in the midst of the garden, and the tree of the knowledge of good and evil. A river flowed out of Eden to water

the garden, and there it divided and became four rivers. The name of
the first is Pishon; it is the one which flows around the whole land of
Havilah, where there is gold; and the gold of that land is good; bdel-
lium and onyx stone are there. The name of the second river is Gihon;
it is the one which flows around the whole land of Cush. And the name
of the third river is Tigris, which flows east of Assyria. And the fourth
river is the Euphrates. The Lord God took the man and put him in the
garden of Eden to till it and keep it.

The reading from the First Epistle of
the Holy Apostle Paul to the Thessalonians. (4:13–18, 5:1–28)

Brethren, we would not have you ignorant concerning those who are
asleep, that you may not grieve as others do who have no hope. For since
we believe that Jesus died and rose again, even so, through Jesus, God
will bring with him those who have fallen asleep. For this we declare to
you by the word of the Lord, that we who are alive, who are left until
the coming of the Lord, shall not precede those who have fallen asleep.
For the Lord himself will descend from heaven with a cry of command,
with the archangel's call, and with the sound of the trumpet of God.
And the dead in Christ will rise first; then we who are alive, who are
left, shall be caught up together with them in the clouds to meet the
Lord in the air; and so we shall always be with the Lord. Therefore comfort one another with these words. But as to the times and the seasons,
brethren, you have no need to have anything written to you. For you
yourselves know well that the day of the Lord will come like a thief in
the night. When people say, "There is peace and security," then sudden
destruction will come upon them as travail comes upon a woman with
child, and there will be no escape. But you are not in darkness, brethren, for that day to surprise you like a thief. For you are all sons of light
and sons of the day; we are not of the night or of darkness. So then let
us not sleep, as others do, but let us keep awake and be sober. For those
who sleep, sleep at night, and those who get drunk are drunk at night.
But, since we belong to the day, let us be sober, and put on the breast-
plate of faith and love, and for a helmet the hope of salvation. For God

has not destined us for wrath, but to obtain salvation through our Lord Jesus Christ, who died for us so that whether we wake or sleep we might live with him. Therefore encourage one another and build one another up, just as you are doing. But we beseech you, brethren, to respect those who labor among you and are over you in the Lord and admonish you, and to esteem them very highly in love because of their work. Be at peace among yourselves. And we exhort you, brethren, admonish the idlers, encourage the fainthearted, help the weak, be patient with them all. See that none of you repays evil for evil, but always seek to do good to one another and to all. Rejoice always, pray constantly, give thanks in all circumstances; for this is the will of God in Christ Jesus for you. Do not quench the Spirit, do not despise prophesying, but test everything; hold fast what is good, abstain from every form of evil. May the God of peace himself sanctify you wholly; and may your spirit and soul and body be kept sound and blameless at the coming of our Lord Jesus Christ. He who calls you is faithful, and he will do it. Brethren, pray for us. Greet all the brethren with a holy kiss. I adjure you by the Lord that this letter be read to all the brethren. The grace of our Lord Jesus Christ be with you.

The reading from the Holy Gospel
according to Saint John. (3:1–21)

At that time, there was a man of the Pharisees, named Nicodemus, a ruler of the Jews. This man came to Jesus by night and said to him, "Rabbi, we know that you are a teacher come from God; for no one can do these signs that you do, unless God is with him." Jesus answered him, "Truly, truly, I say to you, unless one is born anew, he cannot see the kingdom of God." Nicodemus said to him, "How can a man be born when he is old? Can he enter a second time into his mother's womb and be born?" Jesus answered, "Truly, truly, I say to you, unless one is born of water and the Spirit, he cannot enter the kingdom of God. That which is born of the flesh is flesh, and that which is born of the Spirit is spirit. Do not marvel that I said to you, 'You must be born anew.' The wind blows where it wills, and you hear the sound of it, but you do not know whence it comes or whither it goes; so it is with every one who is born of the Spirit." Nicodemus said to him, "How can this be?" Jesus answered him, "Are you a teacher of Israel, and yet you do not understand this? Truly, truly, I say to you, we speak of what we know, and bear witness to what we have seen; but you do not receive our testimony. If I have told you earthly things and you do not believe, how can you believe if I tell you heavenly things? No one has ascended into heaven but he who descended from heaven, the Son of man. And as Moses lifted up the serpent in the wilderness, so must the Son of man be lifted up, that whoever believes in him may have eternal life." For God so loved the world that he gave his only Son, that whoever believes in him should not perish but have eternal life. For God sent the Son into the world, not to condemn the world, but that the world might be saved through him. He who believes in him is not condemned; he who does not believe is condemned already, because he has not believed in the name of the only Son of God. And this is the judgment, that the light has come into the world, and men loved darkness rather than light, because their deeds were evil. For every one who does evil hates the light, and does not come to the light, lest his deeds should be exposed. But he who does what is true comes to the light, that it may be clearly seen that his deeds have been wrought in God.

Glory to Thee O Lord, Glory to Thee.
Let us pray to the Lord.

Prayer for the Departed

O God of spirits and of all flesh, who hast trampled down death and overthrown the devil and given life to thy world: do thou, the same Lord, give rest to the soul of thy departed servant *N.* in a place of brightness, a place of refreshment, a place of repose, whence all sickness, sighing, and sorrow have fled away. Pardon every transgression which *he* has committed, whether by word or deed or thought. For thou art a good God and lovest mankind; because there is no man who lives yet does not sin; for thou only art without sin; thy righteousness is an ever-lasting righteousness, and thy word is truth. For thou art the Resurrection, the Life and the Repose of thy servant *N.* who is fallen asleep, O Christ our God, and unto thee we ascribe glory, together with thy Father who is without beginning, and thine all-holy, good, and life-creating Spirit, now and ever and unto ages of ages. Amen.

Reader: Come, let us worship God our King.
           Come, let us worship and fall down before Christ our King
           and our God.
           Come, let us worship and fall down before Christ himself,
           our King and our God.

PSALM 24

To thee, O Lord, I lift up my soul. O my God, I trust in thee, let me not be put to shame, let not my enemies laugh at me. For all who wait upon thee shall never be put to shame; let those be ashamed who work wickedness. Make known thy ways to me, O Lord, and teach me thy paths. Lead me in thy truth and teach me, for thou art the God of my salvation, on thee I wait all the day. Remember thy compassion, O Lord, and thy mercy, for they are from of old. Do not remember the sins of my youth nor my ignorance, but remember me according to thy mercy, because of thy loving kindness, O Lord. Merciful and upright is the Lord, therefore he will establish the law to guide sinners in the way. The gentle he will guide in justice, the meek he will teach his ways. All the ways of the Lord are mercy and truth for those seeking his covenant and his testimonies. For thy name's sake, O Lord, pardon my iniquity, for it is great. Who is the man that fears the Lord? Him shall God teach in the way he has chosen. His soul shall dwell amidst good things, his seed shall inherit the earth. The Lord is the strength of those who fear him, and he will show them his covenant. My eyes are ever toward the Lord, for he shall pluck my feet out of the net. Look upon me and have mercy on me, for I am an only child and poor. My heart's afflictions have multiplied, bring me out of my distresses. Look on my lowliness and my pain, and forgive all my sins. Look on my enemies, they have multiplied, they hate me with unjustified hatred. Keep my soul and deliver me, let me not be put to shame, for I put my hope in thee. The innocent and the upright cleave to me, for I wait upon thee. Redeem Israel, O God, out of all his troubles.

PSALM 29

I will exalt thee, O Lord, for thou hast upheld me, not letting my foes rejoice over me. O Lord my God, I cried out to thee and thou didst heal me. O Lord, thou hast led my soul out of Hades, thou hast saved me from those going down to the pit. Sing praises to the Lord, you saints of his, and give thanks at the memory of his holiness. For rage is in his anger but in his will there is life; in evening, the weeping sets in but great joy comes in the morning. As for me, I said in my prosperity I shall never be shaken. Lord, by thy will thou gavest strength to my beauty; thou didst hide thy countenance and I was troubled. I shall cry out to thee, O Lord, to the Lord I shall make supplication: What profit is there in my blood when I go down to the pit? Will the dust praise thee? Will it declare thy truth? The Lord heard and had mercy on me, the Lord became my helper. Thou hast turned my lamentation to joy, tearing up my sackcloth and clothing me in gladness that my glory may sing praise to thee, that I not be stunned with sadness. O Lord my God, I will give thanks to thee forever.

PSALM 30

In thee, O Lord, I have hoped, may I never be ashamed, in thy righteousness, deliver and rescue me. Bow down thine ear to me, deliver me speedily; be a God who defends me, a house of refuge to save me. For thou art my strength and my refuge, and for thy name's sake thou wilt guide me and nourish me. For thou wilt set me free from this snare they have hid for me, for thou, O Lord, art my defender. Into thy hands I shall commit my spirit; thou hast redeemed me, O Lord God of truth. Thou hast hated those who guard fiercely their emptiness, but I have hoped in the Lord. I will be glad and rejoice in thy mercy, for thou hast beheld my lowliness, thou hast saved my soul from anguish and didst not imprison me in my enemy's hands, thou hast set my feet in a wide place. Have mercy on me, O Lord, for I am afflicted, my eye is vexed by fury, so are my soul and my stomach. For my life is wasted with grief and my years with groaning, my strength is weakened with poverty, my very bones are vexed. I am the scorn of all my enemies and especially of all my neighbors, I strike fear in all my acquaintances, those seeing me outside all flee from me. I am forgotten as a dead man, out of mind, I am like a broken vessel. For I hear the blame of those who dwell close all around me; when they gather together against me, they scheme to take away my life. But as for me, I have hoped in thee, O Lord, I said: Thou art my God. My times are in thy hands, deliver me from the hand of my enemies and from those who persecute me. Make thy countenance shine upon thy servant, save me in thy mercy. Lead me not into disgrace, O Lord, for I have called upon thee; let the ungodly be disgraced, lead them down into Hades. Let lying lips be put to silence in speaking evil against the righteous with arrogant contempt. How great is thy loving kindness, O Lord, which thou didst hide for those who fear thee, which thou hast wrought for those who hope in thee in the presence of the sons of men. Thou shalt secretly hide them in thy countenance away from men's schemings, thou shalt shelter them in thy tabernacle from the strife of tongues. Blessed be the Lord, for he has made wondrous his mercy in a city under siege. But I had said in my terror, I am cut off, cut off from thy sight—therefore thou didst hear the voice of my prayer when I cried out to thee. O love the Lord, all you his saints, for the Lord seeks out the truth, and those who act in great arrogance he repays in full. Be of good courage and let your heart be strengthened, all you who hope in the Lord.

PSALM 32

Rejoice in the Lord, O you righteous, praise befits the upright. Praise the Lord with the lyre, make music to him on a ten-string harp. Sing to him a new song, chant beautifully to him in jubilation. For the word of the Lord is true and all his works are done in faith. He loves mercy and judgment, the earth is filled with the Lord's mercy. By the Lord's word were the heavens made firm, all their hosts by the breath of his mouth, gathering the seawaters up as into a wineskin, putting the deeps down into storehouses. Let all the earth fear the Lord, let all the world's inhabitants be shaken by him. For he spoke and they came into being, he commanded and they were created. The Lord scatters the counsels of nations, he makes men's thoughts become as nothing, he makes as nothing the counsels of kings. The counsel of the Lord stands forever, the thoughts of his heart unto all generations. Blessed is the nation whose God is the Lord, the people he has chosen as his own inheritance. The Lord looks down from heaven, he sees all the sons of men. From the place he has made to dwell he looks out upon all the earth's peoples, he who alone has fashioned their hearts, who comprehends all their works. A king is not saved by his strong army nor a giant by his immense strength. A horse is a vain hope for safety, nor shall its great strength deliver it. Behold, the eye of the Lord is on those who fear him, on those who hope in his mercy, to deliver their soul from death and to keep them alive in famine. Our soul shall wait for the Lord; he is our helper and defender. For our heart shall rejoice in him because we have hoped in his holy name. Let thy mercy, O Lord, be upon us, as we have set our hope on thee.

PSALM 34

Judge, O Lord, those judging me, make war on those who war against me. Lay hold of weapon and shield and rise up for my help. Draw forth the sword and stop those who pursue me, say to my soul: I am thy salvation. May those seeking out my soul be ashamed and dishonored, may those plotting evil against me be turned back and confounded. May they be like chaff in the wind's face, an angel of the Lord afflicting them. May their way be dark and slippery, an angel of the Lord pursuing them. For without cause they have hidden their snare of corruption for me, for no reason they have reviled my soul. May a snare catch him up unaware, may the trap he has set catch him up, may he fall into his very own trap. And my soul shall be joyful in the Lord, it shall rejoice in his salvation. All my bones shall say: Lord, Lord, who is like thee, delivering the poor from hands stronger than he, the poor and needy from those wrecking him. Unjust witnesses rose up against me, asking me things I knew nothing about. They repaid me evil for good and desolation for my soul. But I, when they assailed me, I put on sackcloth, I humbled my soul with fasting, my prayer would return to my heart. As if he were friend, as if our brother, I would seek to please; like one mourning and saddened, I would be humbled. But they rejoiced in gathering against me, scourges gathered against me and I did not know it, and even when they scattered, they still did not cease; they kept heaping contempt on me, they kept tearing me with their teeth. Lord, when wilt thou look on this? Rescue my soul from their malice, my only-begotten from the lions. I will confess thee in the great assembly, I will praise thee amidst a mighty people. Let them not rejoice over me who are unjustly my enemies, nor let them wink with the eye who hate me without cause. For they spoke peace to me, but in their wrath they schemed and opened wide their mouths at me, saying: Yes, yes! With our own eyes we saw it. But thou, O Lord, hast seen this, do not keep silence. O Lord, do not be far from me. Arise, O Lord, attend to my cause, my God and my Lord, vindicate me. Judge me, O Lord, my God, according to thy righteousness, and let them not rejoice against me. Let them not say in their hearts, yes, yes! Our soul's desire! We have swallowed him up! Let those who rejoice at my woes be ashamed and confounded together, let those shouting contempt at me be clothed with shame and confusion. Let those desiring my righteous cause shout for joy and be glad, saying over and over: may the Lord be magnified who desires his servant's peace. And my tongue shall speak of thy righteousness and of thy praise all the day long.

PSALM 41

As the deer longs for the water brooks, so my soul longs for thee, O my God. My soul thirsts for God, for the living God. When shall I come and appear before the face of God? My tears have been my bread day and night, while they say to me every day, where is your God? I remembered these things and poured out my soul within me, for I shall go into the wondrous tabernacle, even into the house of God, with a voice of rejoicing and praise, the voice of those keeping joyous feast day. Why art thou cast down, O my soul? And why dost thou disquiet me? Hope in God, for I will give thanks to him. He is the salvation of my countenance and my God. My soul within me is troubled, therefore I will remember thee from the land of Jordan and from Hermon's small mountain. Deep calls to deep at the voice of thy cataracts, all thy waves and billows have gone over me. By day the Lord will send his mercy, by night his song shall be with me, a prayer to the God of my life. I will say to God: Thou art my protector, why hast thou forgotten me? Why must I go about all downcast in the afflictions of my enemies? Breaking my bones, my enemies reproached me, saying every day: Where is your God? Why art thou cast down, O my soul? And why dost thou disquiet me? Hope in God, for I will give thanks to him. He is the salvation of my countenance and my God.

PSALM 45

God is our refuge and strength, helper in the afflictions so assailing us. Therefore we will not fear when the earth is shaken, when the mountains are carried down into the sea's depths. Their waters roared and were troubled, the mountains were troubled by his might. The river's rushings gladden God's city, the Most High has hallowed his tabernacle. God is in the midst of her, she shall never be shaken, God shall help her even before the dawn comes. The nations were troubled, kingdoms fell, he uttered his voice, and the earth shook. The Lord of hosts is with us, the God of Jacob is our protector. Come, behold the works of the Lord, the wonders he has wrought on earth, making wars cease on all the earth—for he will break the bow, shatter the weapons, he will burn up the shields in fire. Be still, and know that I am God, I will be exalted among the nations, I will be exalted in the earth. The Lord of hosts is with us, the God of Jacob is our protector.

PSALM 50

Have mercy on me, O God, according to thy great mercy; according to the abundance of thy compassion blot out my transgression. Wash me thoroughly from my iniquity and cleanse me from my sin. For I know my iniquity and my sin is always before me: against thee, thee alone, have I sinned, I have done evil before thee: that thou mayest be justified in thy words and victorious when thou art judged. Behold, I was conceived in iniquities, in sins did my mother conceive me. Behold, thou hast loved the truth, thou hast made manifest to me wisdom's hidden and secret things. Thou shalt sprinkle me with hyssop and I will be made clean, thou shalt wash me and I will be made whiter than snow. Thou shalt make me hear joy and gladness, my humbled bones shall rejoice. Turn thy face from my sins and blot out all my iniquities. Create in me a pure heart, O God, and renew a right Spirit within me. Do not cast me away from thy presence, do not take thy Holy Spirit from me. Restore to me the joy of thy salvation and uphold me by thy guiding Spirit. I will teach transgressors thy ways and the godless shall turn back to thee. Deliver me from bloodguiltiness, O God, the God of my salvation, and my tongue shall rejoice in thy righteousness. O Lord, thou shalt open my lips and my mouth shall declare thy praise. For if thou hadst desired a sacrifice I would have given it; thou wilt not be pleased even with whole burnt sacrifices. A sacrifice to God is a broken spirit, a broken and humbled heart God will not count as nothing. Do good in thy good pleasure to Zion and may Jerusalem's walls be built up. Then thou shalt be pleased with a sacrifice of righteousness, with offering and whole burnt sacrifices, then shall they offer young bulls on thine altar.

PSALM 54

Give ear, O God, to my prayer, do not disdain my supplication, attend to me and hear me. I was depressed in my prayer and troubled by the enemy's voice, by the sinner's oppression, for they turned their iniquity upon me, in wrath they raged against me. My heart was troubled within me, the terror of death has fallen on me. Fear and trembling have come upon me, the darkness has covered me. I said: who will give me wings like a dove, that I may fly away and be at rest? See how far away I have fled, I have dwelt in the wilderness. I was awaiting my savior from faintheartedness and tempest. Drown them in the depths, O Lord, and confuse their tongues, for I have seen iniquity and strife in the city. Day and night it shall surround her, even to her walls, iniquity and toil and unrighteousness are in her midst and usury and deceit have not departed from her streets. For if an enemy had reviled me I would have borne it, if one hating me had bragged against me I would have hidden from him. But it was thou, a man my equal, my guide and my acquaintance, thou that made sweet the meals we shared; in God's house we walked in one mind. Let death come upon them, let them go down alive into hell, for wickedness is in their dwellings, in the very midst of them. As for me, I have cried out to God and the Lord has heard me. Evening and morning and midday I shall tell and proclaim of it, and he shall hear my voice. He will redeem my soul in peace from those closing round me, for in many ways they have pressed me. God will hear and humble them, he who exists before all the ages, for there is no ransom for them, because they have not feared God. He has stretched forth his hand in retribution, they have defiled his covenant. They were scattered by the wrath of his countenance, yet his heart drew near; their words were smoother than oil, yet they were drawn swords. Cast your cares on the Lord and he shall sustain you, he will never permit the righteous to be shaken. But thou, O God, wilt bring them down into the pit of destruction; bloodthirsty and deceitful men shall not live even half their days. As for me, O Lord, I shall hope on thee.

PSALM 103

Bless the Lord, O my soul. O Lord my God, how magnificently dost thou exist, clothed in thanksgiving and majesty, arrayed in light as with a garment, stretching out the heavens like a curtain. He covers his high halls with the waters, appointing the clouds for his staircase, ascending on the wings of the wind, making his angels his spirits, his ministers a flame of fire. He established earth on her sure foundations, she shall never give way unto ages of ages. The deep like a garment is his clothing, the waters shall stand upon the mountains. At thy rebuke they shall flee, at the crash of thy thunder, they shall tremble with fear. The mountains rise up, the valleys sink down, to the place thou hast founded for them. Thou didst set a boundary never to be passed, the waters shall never again cover the earth. Sending the springs into the valleys, he shall make the waters flow between the mountains. They shall give water to every beast, the wild asses shall quench their thirst. The birds of heaven shall dwell by them, from amidst the rocks they shall sing forth. He waters the mountains from his upper chambers. The earth shall be satisfied with the fruit of thy works. Growing the grass for the cattle, raising green plants to serve man, he brings forth bread from the earth and wine to gladden man's heart, oil to make bright his face and bread to strengthen his heart. The trees of the plain shall be fed, the cedars of Lebanon that thou didst plant. In them shall the sparrows make nests, the heron's home greatest among them. On the high hills are the deer, the cliffs are a refuge for the hyrax. He made the moon to mark seasons, the sun knows the time to set. Thou makest darkness and it is night when all the forest beasts will prowl, the young lions roaring for their prey, seeking their food from God. When the sun rises, they will gather and lie down in their dens. Man shall go out to his work and shall labor until the evening. O Lord, how manifold are thy works, in wisdom thou hast made them all. The earth is filled with thy creations, as is this great and spacious sea that teems with countless things, living things both small and great. There the ships ply their way, there is that Leviathan that thou madest to play there. All of them look to thee alone to give them food in due season. When thou givest they shall gather in, when thou openest thy hands everything shall be filled with goodness. But when thou turnest thy face away they shall be deeply troubled, when thou takest their breath away they shall die back again to dust. Thou shalt send forth thy Spirit and they shall be created, thou shalt renew the face of the earth. May the Lord's glory endure forever, the Lord shall be glad in his works. He gazes on the earth and it trembles, he touches mountains and they smoke. I will sing to the Lord all my life, I will sing psalms to my God for as long as I have being. May my thoughts be pleasing to him, and I shall be very glad in the Lord. May the sinners vanish from the earth, may the wicked wholly cease to be. Bless the Lord, O my soul.

PSALM 117

Give thanks to the Lord, for he is good, for his mercy endures forever. Let the house of Israel say he is good, for his mercy endures forever. Let the house of Aaron say he is good, for his mercy endures forever. Let all those who fear the Lord say he is good, for his mercy endures forever. From amidst my affliction I called out to the Lord, and he heard me and led me forth into a large place. The Lord is my helper, I shall never fear what someone could do to me. The Lord is my helper, I shall see my enemies fallen. Better to put trust in the Lord than to trust in men; better to set hope on the Lord than to hope in princes. All the nations surrounded me, but in the name of the Lord I held them at bay, they circled and circled me, but in the name of the Lord I held them at bay, they circled me like bees at a nest, they blazed up like wildfire in dry grass, but in the name of the Lord I held them at bay. Violently shoved, I was going to fall, but the Lord in an instant helped me. The Lord is my strength and my song, he has become my salvation. The joyous sound of salvation is in the tents of the righteous, the right hand of the Lord has worked mightily, the Lord's right hand exalted me, the right hand of the Lord has worked mightily. I shall not die, I shall live and proclaim the works of the Lord. In chastising, the Lord disciplined me, but he did not give me to death. Open to me the gates of righteousness, I shall enter, praising the Lord. This is the gate of the Lord, here the righteous shall enter. I shall give thanks to thee, for thou hast heard me, thou hast become my salvation. The stone that the builders rejected has become the chief cornerstone, and this has come from the Lord, and it is wonderful in our eyes. This is the day the Lord has made, let us rejoice and be glad in it. O Lord, O Lord, save us, help us, O Lord, abundantly. Blessed is he who comes in the name of the Lord, we have blessed all of you from the house of the Lord. God is the Lord and has appeared unto us, celebrate the feast with flourishing boughs, even to the horns of the altar. Thou art my God, I shall give thanks to thee, thou art my God, I shall exalt thee; I shall give thanks to thee, for thou hast heard me and hast become my salvation. Give thanks to the Lord, for he is good, for his mercy endures forever.

PSALM 142

O Lord, hear my prayer, in thy truthfulness heed my plea, answer me in thy righteousness. Do not judge against thy servant, for no man living shall be found to be righteous in thy sight. For the enemy has tormented my soul, he has laid low my life to the earth, making me dwell in dark places like one who has been long dead, and my spirit has fallen into depression, my heart deeply troubled within me. I remembered the days of old, I meditated on all thy works and deeply on the creations of thy hands. I spread out my hands to thee, my soul thirsts like dry land for thee. Hear me speedily, O Lord, my spirit has forsaken me, turn not thy face from me or I shall become like one who goes down into the pit. Grant that I may hear every morning thy mercy for in thee I have hoped, and grant me, O Lord, to know the way wherein I should walk, for I have lifted my soul up to thee. Deliver me, O Lord, from my enemies, for to thee I have fled. Teach me to do thy will, for thou art my God, thy good Spirit shall guide me into the land of uprightness. For thy name's sake, O Lord, thou shalt quicken me to life, in thy righteousness thou shalt bring my soul out from these afflictions. In thy mercy thou shalt destroy my enemies, thou shalt completely unmake all those tormenting my soul, for I am thy servant.

Glory to the Father and to the Son and to the Holy Spirit, now and ever and unto ages of ages. Amen.

Alleluia. Alleluia. Alleluia. Glory to thee, O God. (*thrice*)

Lord, have mercy. (*thrice*)

Sessional Hymns for the Departed
TONE FIVE

Glory to the Father and to the Son and to the Holy Spirit.

Give rest with the righteous to thy servant, O our Savior, and settle *him* in thy courts, as it is written, overlooking, as thou art good, *his* transgressions, whether voluntary or involuntary, and every sin committed in knowledge or in ignorance, O thou who lovest mankind.

Now and ever and unto ages of ages. Amen.

O Christ God who didst shine forth upon the world from a Virgin, through her making us sons of light: have mercy upon us.

The reading from the book of Isaiah. (Isaiah 61)

The Spirit of the Lord God is upon me, because the Lord has anointed me to bring good tidings to the afflicted; he has sent me to bind up the brokenhearted, to proclaim liberty to the captives, and the opening of the prison to those who are bound; to proclaim the year of the Lord's favor, and the day of vengeance of our God; to comfort all who mourn; to grant to those who mourn in Zion—to give them a garland instead of ashes, the oil of gladness instead of mourning, the mantle of praise instead of a faint spirit; that they may be called oaks of righteousness, the planting of the Lord, that he may be glorified. They shall build up the ancient ruins, they shall raise up the former devastations; they shall repair the ruined cities, the devastations of many generations. Aliens shall stand and feed your flocks, foreigners shall be your plowmen and vinedressers; but you shall be called the priests of the Lord, men shall speak of you as the ministers of our God; you shall eat the wealth of the nations, and in their riches you shall glory. Instead of your shame you shall have a double portion, instead of dishonor you shall rejoice in your lot; therefore in your land you shall possess a double portion; yours shall be everlasting joy. For I the Lord love justice, I hate robbery and wrong; I will faithfully give them their recompense, and I will make an everlasting covenant with them. Their descendants shall be known among the nations, and their offspring in the midst of the peoples; all who see them shall acknowledge them, that they are a people whom the

Lord has blessed. I will greatly rejoice in the Lord, my soul shall exult in my God; for he has clothed me with the garments of salvation, he has covered me with the robe of righteousness, as a bridegroom decks himself with a garland, and as a bride adorns herself with her jewels. For as the earth brings forth its shoots, and as a garden causes what is sown in it to spring up, so the Lord God will cause righteousness and praise to spring forth before all the nations.

The reading from the First Epistle of
the Holy Apostle Paul to the Corinthians (15:1–40)

Brethren, now I would remind you in what terms I preached to you the gospel, which you received, in which you stand, by which you are saved, if you hold it fast—unless you believed in vain. For I delivered to you as of first importance what I also received, that Christ died for our sins in accordance with the scriptures, that he was buried, that he was raised on the third day in accordance with the scriptures, and that he appeared to Cephas, then to the twelve. Then he appeared to more than five hundred brethren at one time, most of whom are still alive, though some have fallen asleep. Then he appeared to James, then to all the apostles. Last of all, as to one untimely born, he appeared also to me. For I am the least of the apostles, unfit to be called an apostle, because I persecuted the church of God. But by the grace of God I am what I am, and his grace toward me was not in vain. On the contrary, I worked harder than any of them, though it was not I, but the grace of God which is with me. Whether then it was I or they, so we preach and so you believed. Now if Christ is preached as raised from the dead, how can some of you say that there is no resurrection of the dead? But if there is no resurrection of the dead, then Christ has not been raised; if Christ has not been raised, then our preaching is in vain and your faith is in vain. We are even found to be misrepresenting God, because we testified of God that he raised Christ, whom he did not raise if it is true that the dead are not raised. For if the dead are not raised, then Christ has not been raised. If Christ has not been raised, your faith is futile and you are still in your sins. Then those also who have fallen asleep in

Christ have perished. If for this life only we have hoped in Christ, we are of all men most to be pitied. But in fact Christ has been raised from the dead, the first fruits of those who have fallen asleep. For as by a man came death, by a man has come also the resurrection of the dead. For as in Adam all die, so also in Christ shall all be made alive. But each in his own order: Christ the first fruits, then at his coming those who belong to Christ. Then comes the end, when he delivers the kingdom to God the Father after destroying every rule and every authority and power. For he must reign until he has put all his enemies under his feet. The last enemy to be destroyed is death. "For God has put all things in subjection under his feet." But when it says, "All things are put in subjection under him," it is plain that he is excepted who put all things under him. When all things are subjected to him, then the Son himself will also be subjected to him who put all things under him, that God may be everything to every one. Otherwise, what do people mean by being baptized on behalf of the dead? If the dead are not raised at all, why are people baptized on their behalf? Why am I in peril every hour? I protest, brethren, by my pride in you which I have in Christ Jesus our Lord, I die every day! What do I gain if, humanly speaking, I fought with beasts at Ephesus? If the dead are not raised, "Let us eat and drink, for tomorrow we die." Do not be deceived: "Bad company ruins good morals." Come to your right mind, and sin no more. For some have no knowledge of God. I say this to your shame. But some one will ask, "How are the dead raised? With what kind of body do they come?" You foolish man! What you sow does not come to life unless it dies. And what you sow is not the body which is to be, but a bare kernel, perhaps of wheat or of some other grain. But God gives it a body as he has chosen, and to each kind of seed its own body. For not all flesh is alike, but there is one kind for men, another for animals, another for birds, and another for fish. There are celestial bodies and there are terrestrial bodies; but the glory of the celestial is one, and the glory of the terrestrial is another.

The reading from the Holy Gospel
according to Saint John (4:1–24)

At that time, when the Lord knew that the Pharisees had heard that Jesus was making and baptizing more disciples than John (although Jesus himself did not baptize, but only his disciples), he left Judea and departed again to Galilee. He had to pass through Samaria. So he came to a city of Samaria, called Sychar, near the field that Jacob gave to his son Joseph. Jacob's well was there, and so Jesus, wearied as he was with his journey, sat down beside the well. It was about the sixth hour. There came a woman of Samaria to draw water. Jesus said to her, "Give me a drink." For his disciples had gone away into the city to buy food. The Samaritan woman said to him, "How is it that you, a Jew, ask a drink of me, a woman of Samaria?" For Jews have no dealings with Samaritans. Jesus answered her, "If you knew the gift of God, and who it is that is saying to you, 'Give me a drink,' you would have asked him, and he would have given you living water." The woman said to him, "Sir, you have nothing to draw with, and the well is deep; where do you get that living water? Are you greater than our father Jacob, who gave us the well, and drank from it himself, and his sons, and his cattle?" Jesus said to her, "Every one who drinks of this water will thirst again, but whoever drinks of the water that I shall give him will never thirst; the water that I shall give him will become in him a spring of water welling up to eternal life." The woman said to him, "Sir, give me this water, that I may not thirst, nor come here to draw." Jesus said to her, "Go, call your husband, and come here." The woman answered him, "I have no husband." Jesus said to her, "You are right in saying, 'I have no husband'; for you have had five husbands, and he whom you now have is not your husband; this you said truly." The woman said to him, "Sir, I perceive that you are a prophet. Our fathers worshiped on this mountain; and you say that in Jerusalem is the place where men ought to worship." Jesus said to her, "Woman, believe me, the hour is coming when neither on this mountain nor in Jerusalem will you worship the Father. You worship what you do not know; we worship what we know, for salvation is from the Jews. But the hour is coming, and now is, when the true worshipers will worship the Father in spirit and truth, for such the Father seeks to worship him. God is spirit, and those who worship him must worship in spirit and truth."

Glory to Thee O Lord, Glory to Thee.
Let us pray to the Lord.

The Third Kneeling Prayer of Pentecost

O ever-flowing fountain of life and light, creative power co-eternal with the Father, who hast most excellently fulfilled the whole dispensation of the salvation of mankind, O Christ our God, who didst burst the indestructible bonds of death and the bolts of hell, and hast trampled down the multitude of evil spirits; who didst offer thyself as a blameless victim, giving thine immaculate body as a sacrifice, unblemished and inviolate of all sin, and through that dread and indescribable act of sacrifice didst bestow eternal life upon us; who didst descend into hell and break down its eternal bars, showing forth the way up to those who sat in the lower world; who with allurements of divine wisdom, didst entice the author of evil, the dragon of the abyss, and with cords of gloom didst bind him in hell and in unquenchable fire, confining him in outer darkness by thine infinite might; thou who art the greatly glorified wisdom of the Father, didst manifest thyself as a great helper to the oppressed, enlightening those that sat in darkness and in the shadow of death, thou Lord of eternal glory and beloved Son of the Father most high, Light everlasting of Light everlasting and Sun of righteousness: Hearken to us who pray unto thee, and give rest to the souls of thy servants, our fathers and brethren, who have fallen asleep before us, and our other kinsmen after the flesh, and all thine own who are in the faith, of whom we now make memorial, for in thee is the power over all, and in thy hand thou holdest all the ends of the earth.

Almighty Master, God of the fathers and Lord of mercies, Maker of the race of mortals and immortals and of every nature of man, of that which is brought together and again put asunder, of life and of the end of life, of sojourning here and of translation there, who dost measure the years of life and set the times of death, who bringest down to hell and raisest up, binding in infirmity and releasing unto power, dispensing present things according to need, and ordering those to come as is expedient, quickening with the hope of resurrection those that are smitten with the sting of death: hearken to us, thy humble and piteous servants who pray, and give rest to the souls of thy servants who have fallen asleep before us, in a place of light, in a place of refreshment, in a place of repose, whence all sickness, sorrow, and sighing have fled away; and do thou place their souls in the tabernacles of the righteous, and make them worthy of peace and repose. For the dead praise thee not, neither do those in hell dare to offer thee confession, but we, the living, bless thee, and supplicate thee, and offer for them propitiatory prayers and sacrifices for their souls. O God, who art great and eternal and holy, who lovest mankind and hast vouchsafed us also to stand before thine unapproachable glory, that we may hymn and praise thy wonders: cleanse us, thine unworthy servants, and grant grace that with contrite heart and without presumption, we may offer thee the thrice-holy glorification and thanksgiving for thy great gifts, which thou hast granted and dost ever grant us. O Lord, remember our infirmity, and destroy us not for our transgressions, but be merciful to our humility, that fleeing from the darkness of sin, we may walk in the day of righteousness, and, clothed with the armor of light, may persevere unassailed from every attack of the evil one, so that with boldness we may glorify thee in all things, the only true God and Lover of man. For thine in truth is the great mystery, O Master and Maker of all, both the temporary dissolutions of thy creatures and their restoration thereafter, and eternal rest. We confess thy grace in all things, in our coming into this world, and in our going forth therefrom, which things faithfully pledge unto us, through thine unfailing promise, our hopes of the resurrection and of life incorruptible, which we shall receive hereafter at thy Second Coming. For thou art both the Author of our resurrection and the impartial Judge of those that have lived, and the Lover of man, and the Master and Lord of recompense, who didst partake with us, on equal terms, of flesh and blood, through thine extreme condescension, and of our blameless passions, wherein thou didst willingly submit to temptation, since thou dost possess tenderness and compassion; and, having suffered temptation, thou art become for us who are tempted the helper which thou hadst promised to be, and therefore thou hast led us to thy passionlessness. Accept, therefore, O Master, our prayers and supplications, and give rest to all the fathers and mothers and children, and brothers and sisters of each of us, and to any others of our kindred and of our people, and to every soul that hath gone to rest before in the hope of resurrection unto life eternal. Set their spirits and their names in the book of life, in the bosom of Abraham, Isaac and Jacob, in the land of the living, in the kingdom of heaven, in a Paradise of bliss, leading all, by thy radiant Angels, into thy holy abode, also raising up with thee our bodies in the day which has been appointed according to thy holy and unfailing promise. There is, therefore, O Lord, no death unto thy servants when we go forth from the body and come unto thee, our God, but a change from things most sorrowful unto things most beneficent and most sweet, and rest and joy. And, though we have sinned against thee, be gracious to us and to them, for no one is pure of stain in thy sight, though his life last but one day, except thou alone, who didst reveal thyself sinless on the earth, O Lord Jesus Christ, from whom we all hope to obtain mercy and the forgiveness of sins. Do thou, therefore, as the good God who lovest mankind, remit, forgive, and pardon them and us our offenses, voluntary and involuntary, done with knowledge or in ignorance, manifest or unnoticed, of deed, of thought, of word, and of all our acts and movements. And to those who have been taken from us give freedom and respite. Bless us who are here present, granting a good and peaceful ending to us and to all thy people, and open to us thy tender mercies and thy love for man at thy dread and fearful Second Coming, and make us worthy of thy kingdom. For thou art the repose of our souls and bodies, and to thee do we send up glory, to the Father, and to the Son, and to the Holy Spirit, now and ever, and unto ages of ages. Amen.

If the preparation is not concluded at this time, begin the reading of the Psalter with Psalm 1 or repeat the psalms herein.

Concluding Prayers

Holy God, holy mighty, holy immortal: have mercy on us. (*thrice*)

Glory to the Father and to the Son and to the Holy Spirit, now and ever and unto ages of ages. Amen.

All-holy Trinity, have mercy on us. Lord, cleanse us from our sins. Master, pardon our transgressions. Holy One, visit and heal our infirmities for thy Name's sake.

Lord, have mercy. (*thrice*)

Glory to the Father and to the Son and to the Holy Spirit, now and ever and unto ages of ages. Amen.

Our Father, who art in heaven, hallowed be thy Name; thy kingdom come; thy will be done, on earth as it is in heaven. Give us this day our daily bread, and forgive us our trespasses as we forgive those who trespass against us; and lead us not into temptation, but deliver us from the evil one.

Priest, if present: For thine is the kingdom and the power and the glory of the Father and of the Son and of the Holy Spirit, now and ever and unto ages of ages. Amen.

Or reader: Through the prayers of our holy Fathers, O Lord Jesus Christ our God, have mercy on us and save us. Amen.

Lord, have mercy. (*twelve times*)

Priest, if present: Wisdom! Most holy Theotokos, save us.

People: More honorable than the Cherubim and more glorious beyond compare than the Seraphim: without corruption thou gavest birth to God the Word, true Theotokos we magnify thee.

Glory to the Father and to the Son and to the Holy Spirit, now and ever and unto ages of ages. Amen.

Lord, have mercy. (*thrice*)

Father, bless. *or* Bless, O Lord.

Priest or reader: O Lord Jesus Christ our God, through the prayers of thine All-pure Mother, of our venerable and God-bearing Fathers, of Saints Joseph and Nicodemus together with the holy Myrrh-bearing Women, of the holy, glorious, and all-laudable Apostles and of all the saints, have mercy on us and save us. Amen.

Priest, if present: Grant rest eternal and blessed repose, O Lord, to the soul of thy newly-departed servant *N.,* and make *his* memory to be eternal.

People: Memory eternal. (*thrice*)

In conclusion, those who
prepared the body ask forgiveness:

Beloved *brother* in Christ, *N.,* forgive us if at any time we have offended you by anything we have done or have left undone. May your memory be eternal.

Appendix A

Contents of the Preparation Kit

THE CHURCH SHOULD PREPARE a supply kit for this ministry and have a suitable, centralized place to keep it so that it is easily accessible in an emergency should the pastor or team leader be out of town. If the concept of a return to ancient Christian burial takes hold in your community, then several churches can combine resources and team members. Team leaders may want to keep their own kits as well. An old airline carryon size suitcase, from the local thrift shop or your attic, should work just fine. On the next page is a check-list to help you get started. Add or substitute items as your experience suggests ways to improve this list.

A note on annointing oil: Light olive oil (*virgin* not *extra-virgin*) mixed with essential oils such as myrrh, frankincense, or sandalwood (120 drops essential oil per 8 oz. carrier oil). We are not required to use olive oil, but it is more traditional. "Cold pressed" olive oil is preferred by professionals. Myrrh and sandalwood can be effective antibacterial agents but we shouldn't count on this when using olive oil as the carrier. Frankincense and sandalwood are often used in aroma therapy to relieve grief, stress, anxiety, depression, and fear; all of which are associated with funerals and dead bodies. Essential oils are generally available from aroma therapists, health spas, your local "new age" emporium or on the internet. Always handle essential oils with caution as they are very potent.

KEEP THEM AWAY FROM CHILDREN!

Avoid using essential oils such as ajowan, almond bitter, and others listed as hazardous.

More information on essential oils is available at your local library or on the Internet.

A dark plastic eight ounce pharmacy bottle is perfect for anointing oil. We have it blessed and keep one ready in the kit at all times. Keep it in a plastic bag just in case it leaks.

Preparation Kit Contents List

A copy of this handbook
Cross or Icon (diptych or triptych)
Candle (luminary in glass or
    plastic)
Censer, incense, charcoal, and
    lighter
New Testament and Psalms
Surgical gloves (box or
    partial box)
Wet wipes
Antibacterial cleanser
Wash cloths or sponges (2–3)
Sponges for anointing (2–3)
Plastic basin
Shampoo
Anointing Oil Mix (8 oz)
Hair brush
Comb
Blow dryer
Three towels
Ring Cutter
Dental floss (ring remover)
4 x 4 gauze pads

Plastic bags (to hold wet cloths)
Plastic sheet or bed protector
White bed sheets (2–3)
Extra large T-shirts (2–3)
Six bed pads (disposable)
Trash bags (for bed pads, etc.)
Disposable diapers (2–3)
Cloth diapers (2–3)
Tampons (2–3)
Small tube of petroleum jelly
Small jar menthol rub
Q-tips
Long tweezers
Manicure set
Cotton balls
Rolled bandages for binding
Eye pillow (bean bag)
Ribbon or scarf for mouth
Small pillow for under chin
Super glue
Baptismal garment
Burial shroud
Portable recording and player

Appendix B

Postmortem Legal Forms

1. A Gift for My Loved Ones
        (Estate Planning Documents)
        Healthcare Power of Attorney
        Advance Directive for Healthcare
2. Another Gift for My Loved Ones
        (Funeral Planning Documents)
        Advance Directive for Funeral Care
        Burial and Funeral Care Instructions

A Gift

For My
Loved
Ones

This package contains everything you need to know if I am disabled,
or incapacitated and cannot make decisions for myself.
It includes my Health Care Power of Attorney and
Advance Directive for Health Care - Living Will

Dear Loved Ones,

It's hard to think about death. We cling so hard to the temporary pleasures of this life that sometimes we forget our true life; life in Christ. My life with you has been a gift from God. Through all the struggles, pain and great joy I have been loved by you and always by God. As an Orthodox Christian I've always known that our true home is with Christ There will be no sorrow, no sadness and no loss, only love and joy when we are all together with our Lord.

Long ago I placed my life entirely in the hands of our gracious Lord. I know there are many things that I can't control, but there are several things that it's not only my option but also my duty to control. If I should be in an accident or otherwise incapacitated I know it would be very stressful for my loved ones to make the hard decisions that might need to be made. So I'm taking the hard step of thinking about these things myself so that you know how I would make these decisions and what I would want you to do.

In the following pages I will name a person to hold primary Health Care Power of Attorney and an alternate. I will give that person authority to make those hard decisions and direction by my own wishes. In another document I'll name someone to make funeral arrangements for me through my Advance Directive for Funeral Care and I will give them guidance as to my wishes with my funeral planning form.

In the event that I am gravely or terminally ill or in a state of diminished consciousness so that I can't make decisions for myself, I direct that decisions be made for me that are in conformity with the beliefs and tenets of the Eastern Orthodox Christian Church, some of which are outlined below. I request that an Orthodox priest be contacted to visit with me, hear confession and bring communion for some time prior to my death. When my death is near I request him to be present so that I might make a final confession of my sins and partake of the prayers and sacraments of the church. I also request that Orthodox Prayers for the Newly Departed be said immediately after my death.

My Orthodox Christian beliefs hold that it is unethical to take a life. While it is not the highest of all values to preserve life, affirmative steps to cause death, including but not limited to euthanasia or suicide, are not blessed by the Church. However, it can be permissible, and even appropriate, to allow nature to take its course without extraordinary medical intervention, until God determines to take my life. Using extraordinary medical measures to merely maintain my body's biological functioning may not be appropriate. My death, if with dignity and with proper respect for the rites and traditions of the church, can be a victory of faith.

The Orthodox Church does not condone Physician Assisted Suicide, removing artificial nutrition/hydration from a patient who is conscious but unable to communicate, nor removing artificial nutrition/hydration from a patient who has severe dementia but otherwise has no other acute health problems. However, I also recognize that , as one begins the dying process, forced nutrition/hydration do not help but can interfere with the process and can cause great discomfort. In this case, with the approval of my Agent and my doctors, nutrition/hydration may be withdrawn in favor of proper maintenance of my mucus membranes for my comfort.

Any type of Physicians order for Life Sustaining Treatment signed by a physician or my Agent must be consistent with the contents of my directives contained here.

The original of this form should be with the Agent named on this document. A copy should be with the alternate Agent named, and a copy on file with my church or burial society. Other copies should be distributed to my spouse, children, parents and/or any others who might need to know this information. A copy should be supplied to any hospital, nursing home, rehabilitation center, assisted living or other health care facility that I may enter. I do this to help avoid any confusion over who I have authorized to make decisions regarding my healthcare and my remains after my death.

If I become incapacitated and unable to make my own healthcare decisions I name the following person(s) to make those decisions on my behalf based on my Orthodox Christian beliefs. The judgment of my incapacity to make health decisions must be made and agreed to by at least two medical physicians who have personally examined me.

I understand that this document gives the person(s) I name as my agent the power to make health care decisions for me if I can't make the decisions for myself. This power includes the power to make decisions about life-sustaining treatment. In the event of my incapacity my agent will have the same authority to make decisions about my healthcare as I would have. My agent will be obligated to follow my instructions when making decisions on my behalf. After I have signed this document, I have the right to make health care decisions for myself if I am mentally competent to do so. After I have signed this document, no treatment may be given to me or stopped over my objection if I am mentally competent to make that decision. I have the right to revoke this document, and terminate my agent's authority, by informing either my agent or my health care provider in writing.

This Healthcare power of attorney will not be valid unless two persons sign as witnesses and a Notary Public is present to witness all our signatures.

The following persons may NOT act as witnesses:

1. A person who is directly financially responsible for my medical care.
2. A person who is named in my will, or, if I have no will, who would inherit my property by intestate succession.
3. A beneficiary of a life insurance policy on my life.
4. The persons named in the Health Care Power of Attorney as my agent or successor agent.
5. My physician or an employee of my physician.
6. Any person who would have a claim against any portion of my estate (persons to whom I owe money).

If I am a patient in a health facility, no more than one witness may be an employee of that facility.

My agent to whom I grant Healthcare Power of Attorney must be a person who is 18 years old or older and of sound mind. It may not be my doctor or any other health care provider that is now providing me with treatment or an employee of my doctor or provider; or a spouse of the doctor, provider, or employee; unless the person is a relative of mine.

I understand that this letter to my loved ones is only explanatory. The terms and conditions of my Healthcare Power of Attorney and Living Will shall govern.

With love,

Contact List:

1. Local Church and priest:_____ phone:_____

2. Alternate Church and priest:_____ phone:_____

3. Power of Attorney: _____ phone:_____

HEALTH CARE POWER OF ATTORNEY

I - Designation of Health Care Agent

I, _____, being of sound mind and body, do hereby appoint the following as my health care attorney-in-fact (herein referred to as my "health care agent") to act for me and in my name (in any way I could act in person) to make health care decisions for me as authorized in this document:

Agent Name: _____
Address:_____

Cellular Telephone: _____ Home Telephone: _____

In the event that _____, ceases to act as my health care agent due to death, incapacity, resignation, divorce or separation, I hereby appoint the person named below as my alternate health care agent.
Alternate Agent Name: _____
Address:_____
Cellular Telephone: _____Home Telephone:_____

II - Effectiveness of Appointment

Absent revocation, the authority granted in this document shall become effective when and if my attending physician and one other physician who has personally examined me shall determine that I lack sufficient understanding or capacity to make or communicate decisions relating to my health care, including mental health treatment, and will continue in effect during my incapacity, until my death, except if I authorize my health care agent to exercise my rights with respect to anatomical gifts, autopsy, or disposition of my remains, this authority will continue after my death to the extent necessary to exercise the authority granted in this document for these purposes; provided, however, that paragraph I of Section III following shall be effective upon the signing of this document and is not dependent upon my incapacity. This determination shall be made by my then treating physician.

III - General Statement of Authority Granted

Except as indicated in section IV below, I hereby grant to my health care agent named above full power and authority to make health care decisions, including mental health treatment decisions on my behalf, including, but not limited to, the following:

A. To request, review, and receive any information, verbal or written, regarding my physical or mental health, including, but not limited to, medical and hospital records, and to consent to the disclosure of this information;

B. To employ or discharge my health care providers;

C. To consent to and authorize my admission to and discharge from a hospital, nursing or convalescent home, or other institution;

D. To consent to and authorize my admission to and retention in a facility for the care or treatment of mental illness;

E. To give consent to and authorize the administration of medications for mental health treatment but not electro-convulsive treatment (ECT) commonly referred to as "shock treatment;"

F. To give consent for, to withdraw consent for, or to withhold consent for, X ray, anesthesia, medication, surgery, and all other diagnostic and treatment procedures ordered by or under the authorization of a licensed physician, dentist, or podiatrist. This authorization specifically includes the power to consent to measures for relief of pain;

G. To authorize the withholding or withdrawal of life-sustaining procedures when and if my physicians determine I have a condition that is incurable or irreversible and, without the administration of life-sustaining procedures, expected to result in death within a relatively short period of time; or if I am in a state of permanent unconsciousness. Life-sustaining procedures are those forms of medical care that serve only to artificially prolong the dying process and may include mechanical ventilation, dialysis, antibiotics, and other forms of medical treatment which sustain, restore or supplant vital bodily functions. Life-sustaining treatments could also include artificial nutrition and hydration when the conditions above are met, and they are only prolonging the dying process.

H. To exercise any right that I may have to make a disposition of any part of my body for medical purposes: to authorize an autopsy only if required by law; to make an anatomical gift of my organs or part thereof, but not my whole body; and to direct the disposition of my remains according to the rites and teachings of the canonical Orthodox Christian faith; and

I. I intend for my agent named above to be treated as I would be with respect to my rights regarding the use and disclosure of my individually identifiable health information or other medical records. This release authority applies to any information governed by the Health Insurance Portability and Accountability Act of 1996 (a.k.a. HIPAA), 42 U.S.C .1320d and 45 C.F.R. 160-164. I authorize: any physician, health care professional, dentist, health plan, hospital, clinic, laboratory, pharmacy or other covered health care provider, any insurance company and the Medical Information Bureau, Inc. or other health care clearinghouse that has provided treatment or services to me, or that has paid for or is seeking payment from me for such services, to give, disclose and release to my agent, without restriction, all of my individually identifiable health information and medical records regarding any past, present or future medical or mental health condition, including all information relating to the diagnosis and treatment of HIV/AIDS, sexually transmitted diseases, mental illness, and drug or alcohol abuse. The authority given my agent shall supersede any prior agreement that I may have made with my health care providers to restrict access to or disclosure of my individually identifiable health information. The authority granted under this HIPAA Release is effective immediately. The authority given my agent has no expiration date and shall expire only in the event that I revoke the authority in writing and deliver it to my health care provider. and

J. To take any lawful actions that may be necessary to carry out these decisions, including the granting of releases of liability to medical providers.

IV - Special Provisions and Limitations

A. In exercising the authority to make health care decisions on my behalf, the authority of my health care agent is subject to the following special provisions and limitations: he shall not allow

Physician Assisted Suicide, removing artificial nutrition/hydration from me if I am conscious but unable to communicate, nor removing artificial nutrition/hydration from me if I have severe dementia but otherwise have no other acute health problems.

B. In exercising the authority to make mental health decisions on my behalf, the authority of my health care agent is subject to the following special provisions and limitations: My health care agent may not consent to nor authorize the administration of electroconvulsive treatment (ECT), commonly referred to as "shock treatment;"

C. I have executed a Living Will and it is my direction that my health care agent act consistently with my instructions in the Living Will. In the event of a conflict between the instructions contained in my Living Will and the instructions of my health care agent, it is my desire and intention that the provisions of my Living Will should control; and

D. In exercising the authority to make decisions regarding autopsy, anatomical gifts and disposition of remains on my behalf, the authority of my health care agent is subject to the following special provisions and limitations: no autopsy shall be performed unless it is required by law, no whole body donation. *(Initial one below)*

_____   Organ donations are allowable.
_____   No organ donation.

Other _____

V - Guardianship Provision

If it becomes necessary for a court to appoint a guardian of my person, I nominate my health care agent acting under this document to be the guardian of my person, to serve without bond or security. The guardian shall act consistently with provisions of this State's laws.

VI - Reliance of Third Parties on Health Care Agent

A. No person who relies in good faith upon the authority of or any representations by my health care agent shall be liable to me, my estate, my heirs, successors, assigns, or personal representatives, for actions or omissions by my health care agent; and

B. The powers conferred on my health care agent by this document may be exercised by my health care agent alone, and my health care agent's signature or act under the authority granted in this document may be accepted by persons as fully authorized by me and with the same force and effect as if I were personally present, competent, and acting on my own behalf. All acts performed in good faith by my health care agent pursuant to this power of attorney are done with my consent and shall have the same validity and effect as if I were present and exercised the powers myself, and shall inure to the benefit of and bind me, my estate, my heirs, successors, assigns, and personal representatives. The authority of my health care agent pursuant to this power of attorney shall be superior to and binding upon my family, relatives, friends and others.

C. Any party dealing with my alternate health care agent may rely upon his representation as to my original health care agent's death, incapacity or resignation as conclusively correct. A copy of this form shall be as good as the original.

VII - Miscellaneous Provisions

A. I revoke any prior health care power of attorney;

B. My health care agent shall be entitled to sign, execute, deliver, and acknowledge any contract or other document that may be necessary, desirable, convenient or proper in order to exercise and carry out any of the powers described in this document and to incur reasonable costs on my behalf incident to the exercise of these powers; provided, however, that except as shall be necessary in order to exercise the powers described in this document relating to my health care, my health care agent shall not have any authority over my property or financial affairs;

C. My health care agent and my health care agent's estate, heirs, successors, and assigns are hereby released and forever discharged by me, my estate, my heirs, successors, and assigns and personal representatives from all liability and from all claims or demands of all kinds arising out of the acts or omissions of my health care agent pursuant to this document, except for willful misconduct or gross negligence; and

D. No act or omission of my health care agent, or of any other person, institution, or facility acting in good faith in reliance on the authority of my health care agent pursuant to this health care power of attorney shall be considered suicide, nor the cause of my death for any civil or criminal purposes, nor shall it be considered unprofessional conduct or as a lack of professional competence. Any person, institution, or facility against whom criminal or civil liability is asserted because of conduct authorized by this health care power of attorney may interpose this document as a defense.

VIII - Signature of Principal

By signing here, I indicate that I am mentally alert and competent, fully informed as to the contents of this document, and understand the full import of this grant of powers to my health care agent.

_____   _____ (SEAL)
Date   Signature of Principal

STATE OF _____

COUNTY OF _____

I, _____, a Notary Public for _____County, _____ hereby certify that _____appeared before me and swore to me and to the Witnesses in my presence that this instrument is a Health Care Power of Attorney, and that he/she willingly and voluntarily made and executed it as his/her free act and deed for the purposes expressed in it.

This the _____ day of _____, 20_____.

Notary Public:_____My Commission Expires: _____

IX - Signature of Witnesses

I hereby state that the Principal, _____, being of sound mind, signed the foregoing health care power of attorney in my presence, and that I am not related to the principal by blood or marriage, and I would not be entitled to any portion of the estate of the principal under any existing Will or Codicil of the principal or as an heir under any law regulating intestate succession in this state, if the principal died on this date without a Will. I also state that I am not the principal's attending physician, nor an employee of the principal's attending physician, nor an employee of a nursing home or any group care home where the principal resides. I further state that I do not have any claim against the principal.

_____   _____

Date   Witness 1

_____   _____

Date   Witness 2

STATE OF _____

COUNTY OF _____

I hereby certify that _____ and _____, Witnesses, are personally known to me or have provided proper identification and appeared before me and swore that they witnessed _____sign the attached Health Care Power of Attorney, believing him/her to be of sound mind; and also swore that at the time they witnessed the signing (i) they were not related within the third degree to him/her or his/her spouse, and (ii) they did not know nor have a reasonable expectation that they would be entitled to any portion of his/her estate upon his/her death under any Will or Codicil thereto then existing or under any law regulating intestate succession in this state, as it provided at that time, and (iii) they were not a physician attending to him/her, nor an employee of an attending physician, nor an employee of a health facility in which he/she was a patient, nor an employee of a nursing home or any group-care home in which he/she resided, and (iv) they did not have a claim against him/her. I further certify that I am satisfied as to the genuineness and due execution of the instrument.

This the ___ day of _____, 201___.

Notary Public:_____My Commission Expires: _____

DECLARATION OF A DESIRE FOR A NATURAL DEATH

I, _____, of (Town) _____, [State]_____, believe it is important to make known my decision regarding the administration and continuation of any medical procedure or intervention that would serve only to postpone the moment of my death. To this end I am making the following declaration.

I am of sound mind and at least eighteen years of age. I direct that my life shall not be artificially prolonged under the circumstances set forth below and hereby declare that:

If at any time my attending physician and one other physician who has personally examined me certify in writing that I am: (initial all those that apply)

_____ Permanently unconscious with a ventilator breathing for me;

_____ Permanently unconscious with a feeding tube and/or intravenous (IV) hydration;

_____ Maintained on a ventilator when there is little or no chance for recovery;

_____ or In any other permanent and terminal medical condition due to which the application of life sustaining treatment would serve only to artificially prolong the process of dying or maintain me in the permanent medical condition, then;

I direct that life-sustaining procedures shall be withdrawn and withheld pursuant to the terms of this declaration, it being understood that life-sustaining procedures shall not include any medical procedure or intervention for nourishment and hydration considered necessary by the attending physician to provide comfort or alleviate pain. The life-sustaining procedures which may be withheld or withdrawn include, but are not limited to: surgery, antibiotics, cardiac resuscitation, respiratory support, chemotherapy, radiation, dialysis and transfusions, and other forms of medical treatment which sustain, restore or supplant vital bodily functions.

I seek treatment only to keep me comfortable, even if such treatment may shorten my life.

Note: Physician Assisted Suicide is prohibited. Removing artificial nutrition/hydration if I am conscious but unable to communicate but otherwise have no other acute health problems is prohibited. Removing artificial nutrition/ hydration if I have severe dementia but otherwise have no other acute health problems is prohibited.

However, I may specifically direct that artificial nourishment be withdrawn or withheld pursuant to the terms of this declaration above. "Artificial nourishment" means nourishment supplied by means of a naso-gastric tube or tube inserted into the stomach or intestines, or nutrients injected intravenously into the bloodstream.

With respect to Nutrition and Hydration, I direct that in situations where life-sustaining treatments are being withheld or withdrawn pursuant to conditions above (INITIAL **ONLY ONE** OF THE FOLLOWING THREE PARAGRAPHS):

_____Artificial nourishment shall not be continued; or

_____Artificial nourishment shall be continued; or

_____Artificial nourishment shall be continued until such time as my Agent and two (2) physicians who have personally examined me determine that the dying process has begun and continuation of nutrition/hydration would only cause me discomfort.

In the event my physicians certify my condition as terminal, my physician may discharge his or her obligation of notice by notifying my Health Care Agent or any successor Health Care Agent serving under my Health Care Power of Attorney.

This instrument is made and given in the full knowledge that I can rely on the love and affection of my relatives and friends and with thankfulness that they will understand my reasons.

This the ____ day of _____, 20____.   _____
                                                    [Principal Signature], Declarant

I hereby state that the declarant, _____, being of sound mind, signed the above declaration in my presence and that I am not related to the declarant by blood or marriage and that I do not know or have a reasonable expectation that I would be entitled to any portion of the estate of the declarant under any existing Will or Codicil of the declarant or as an heir under any law regulating intestate succession in this state, if the declarant died on this date without a Will. I also state that I am not the declarant's attending physician or an employee of the declarant's attending physician, or an employee of a health facility in which the declarant is a patient or an employee of a nursing home or any group-care home where the declarant resides. I further state that I do not now have any claim against the declarant.

_____ residing at _____
        Witness 1

_____ residing at _____
        Witness 2

STATE OF _____

COUNTY OF _____

I, _____, a Notary Public for the County of _____, State of _____, hereby certify that _____, the declarant, appeared before me and swore to me and to the Witnesses in my presence that this instrument is Declaration of a Desire for a Natural Death, and that he/she had willingly and voluntarily made and executed it as a free act and deed for the purposes expressed in it.

I further certify that _____and _____,
Witnesses, personally known to me or providing proper identification appeared before me and swore that they witnessed _____, declarant, sign the attached declaration, believing him/her to be of sound mind; and also swore that at the time they witnessed the declaration (i) they were not related within the third degree to the declarant or to the declarant's spouse, and (ii) they did not know or have a reasonable expectation that they would be entitled to any portion of the estate of the declarant upon the declarant's death under any Will of the declarant or Codicil thereto then existing or under any law regulating intestate succession in this state, as it provides at that time, and (iii) they were not a physician attending the declarant or an employee of an attending physician or an employee of a health facility in which the declarant was a patient or an employee of a nursing home or any group-care home in which the declarant resided, and (iv) they did not have a claim against the declarant. I further certify that I am satisfied as to the genuineness and due execution of the declaration.

This the ____ day of _____, 20____.

Notary Public: _____ My Commission Expires:_____

Another Gift

For My Loved Ones

> This package contains everything
> you need to know to arrange
> my funeral and burial.

Dear Loved Ones,

Here I have done the hard work so that you don't have to.

The following pages provide information for my designated agent to use in making arrangements for my funeral and burial. You do not need to use a funeral director if you choose not to. There are NO states in the US that require embalming. Only eight states require you to use a funeral director at all.

On the following page I have named an agent and alternates and given them exclusive authority to see that the instructions in this document are followed to the best of their ability and according to existing law. I have signed this document in the presence of two witnesses and a notary public. The information provided here will inform them and you of:

1) How I would like my burial to be handled

2) Who I would like to handle different aspects of the funeral and burial

3) Other information to assist those persons in carrying out my wishes

4) A list of people to notify of my death

5) Information for my obituary

6) Information about the location of important papers such as Last Will and Testament, birth certificates, financial documents, insurance policies, military records etc. which will be useful to my family and the executor of my Will.

(DO NOT place any of these important papers in a safe deposit box. The box will be sealed upon my death.)

The original copy of my Funeral Instructions can be found in the following

location:_____

These people hold a copy of my Funeral Instructions:

Name_____Phone:_____

Name_____Phone:_____

Name_____Phone:_____

Name_____Phone:_____

Date:_____

Signature:_____

ADVANCE DIRECTIVE FOR FUNERAL CARE
DEATH-CARE POWER OF ATTORNEY

Be it known to all parties that I,_____ , am an
Orthodox Christian of sound mind and I direct that my remains be treated in a traditional Orthodox Christian
manner.

I hereby direct (Name)_____ , (address) _____ ,
(phone #s) _____ at his/her/their discretion to make any and all
arrangements for the care and disposition of my bodily remains after my death as directed in the following pages
of this document. Should he/she pre-decease me, or for any other reason be unable to fulfill this responsibility, I
designate and direct _____(address) _____ ,
(phone #s)_____ to make any and all arrangements regarding the care and
disposition of my bodily remains upon my death as directed in a subsequent document. A copy shall be as good
as the original.

Absolutely NO AUTOPSY shall be performed unless required by law.

☐ I AM   ☐ AM NOT an organ donor

Neither doctors, hospitals, nursing homes, hospice, coroner nor any other person or entity in whose care I may be
has any authority to make any arrangements, including calling a funeral home, for any reason before contacting the
person(s) named above to be advised by that person of my wishes concerning the disposition of my bodily remains
after my death. The above-named parties should be contacted promptly if death is imminent or expected.

Signature_____ date_____ SEAL
Address:_____ Phone:_____

Witness 1_____ date_____ SEAL
Address:_____ Phone:_____

Witness 2_____ date_____ SEAL
Address:_____ Phone:_____

STATE OF_____ COUNTY OF _____

On this ____ day of _____ , 20____ the said _____ (principal),
_____ , and _____(witnesses) known to
me (or satisfactorily proven) to be the person named in ther foregoing instrument and witnesses, respectively,
personally appeared before me, a Notary Public within the State and County aforesaid, and acknowledged that
they freely and voluntarily executed the same for the purposes stated therein.

My commission expires _____   _____
                                              Notary Public

ADVANCE DIRECTIVE
Burial and Funeral Care Instructions

My Legal Name:_____

Name:_____
As you want it to appear in the newspaper notice
Address:_____

Home Phone:_____Work_____   Occupation_____

Birth Place:_____   Birth Date_____

Marital Status: Single_____Married_____   Divorced_____Widowed_____

Father's Name:_____   Mother's Maiden Name_____

Nearest Relative:_____   Executor:_____

Relationship:_____   Relationship:_____

Address:_____   Address:_____

_____   _____

Home Phone:_____Work_____   Home Phone:_____Work_____

Legal Guardian of Minor Children:_____

Address:_____

Home Phone:_____   Work Phone:_____

I, _____, being of sound mind and under no restraint, hereby direct that the following instructions and preferences be honored after my death:

I direct that my funeral preparation, funeral and burial be conducted according to the rites, traditions and practices of the Holy Orthodox Church.

☐ I prefer a home and church funeral with minimum or no mortuary involvement.

☐ I prefer a mortuary: (mortuary name)_____

Have arrangements been made with the mortuary?: ☐ YES ☐ NO   Paid? ☐ YES ☐ NO

If paid, payment records can be found _____

Embalming: ☐ YES   ☐ NO

Clothing: indicate first (1) and second (2) preference: (   )From existing wardrobe (   )Plain white garment provided by church   ☐ WITH   ☐ WITHOUT Printed burial shroud   Headband. circle Yes   No

OTHER:_____

Items to be interred with the body or removed (specify items and where they can be found or to whom they are to be delivered (wedding ring, watch, cross, earrings, etc.):_____
_____

Preferred cemetery or burial site (indicate first (1) and second (2) preferences):_____
_____

Have arrangements been made with the cemetery: ☐ YES ☐ NO

Prefered type of grave marker (must meet cemetery requirements):_____

Preferred inscription on grave marker:_____

Names of pallbearers (provide contact information on a different sheet):_____

Other instructions: (organ donations, flowers, other memorial donations, etc):_____

_____

_____

I direct that the person or organizations named below perform or coordinate the following services:

Notify relatives: ☐ Church ☐ Executor ☐ Other (specify):_____

Prepare body for burial (washing and clothing body if not embalmed):

 ☐ Church ☐ Mortuary ☐ Family ☐ Other (specify)_____

Provide Casket:

 ☐ Church ☐ Mortuary ☐ Family ☐ Other (specify)_____

Take care of administrative details (death certificate, etc.):

 ☐ Church ☐ Mortuary ☐ Other (specify)_____

Prepare and publish obituary:

 ☐ Church ☐ Mortuary ☐ Other (specify)_____

Transport Body to mortuary or church:

 ☐ Church ☐ Mortuary ☐ Other (specify)_____

Transport body to cemetery: ☐ Church ☐ Mortuary ☐ Other (specify)_____

Obtain and install grave marker: ☐ Church ☐ Family/Executor ☐ Other (specify)_____

Other Services:

Temporary Child care: ☐ Church ☐ Executor ☐ Family ☐ Other (specify)_____

Interim care of pets: ☐ Church ☐ Executor ☐ Family ☐ Other (specify)_____

Temporary Housing arrangements for relatives: ☐ Church ☐ Executor ☐ Family

 ☐ Other (specify)_____

(Optional) I have provided financial information and the location of important records to:

 ☐ Church ☐ Executor ☐ Other (specify) _____

I have previously filed instructions for funeral arrangements: YES NO

If YES: They are located:_____

 The previous instructions are hereby cancelled: YES NO

 The previous instructions supplement this form: YES NO

Payment for funeral costs:

 Has already been made to _____

 Receipts and pertinent papers are located:_____

 Should be paid from my estate.

 I desire and direct that any savings on funeral expenses due to Church or funeral society

 involvement be donated to _____

PEOPLE TO BE NOTIFIED OF MY DEATH

Name	Address	Phone	Relationship

OBITUARY INFORMATION

Date of Birth:_____

Place of Birth: City_____State _____County _____

Resident of _____County since _____.

Father's Name/Birthplace (living or deceased?)_____

Mother's Maiden Name/Birthplace (living or deceased?)_____
_____

Spouses Name(s) (living or deceased?)_____
_____

Children (living or deceased?)_____
_____
_____
_____

Other Relatives (living or deceased?)_____
_____
_____
_____

Occupation/Employer_____

Veteran: ☐ YES ☐ NO Branch of service_____Serial No:_____
    Veterans Affairs Claim Number_C-_____
    Rank_____
    Name of war or dates served_____
    Service Awards/Decorations_____

EDUCATION, ETC.
High School_____Diploma/GED_____Year_____

College/University_____Degrees Earned_____Year_____

College/University_____Degrees Earned_____Year_____

College/University_____Degrees Earned_____Year_____

Club/ Fraternal Civic Organization_____

Offices Held_____

Club/ Fraternal Civic Organization_____

Offices Held_____

Club/ Fraternal Civic Organizations_____

Offices Held_____

Hobbies_____

Awards_____

Additional Information_____

_____

_____

_____

_____

_____

_____

_____

_____

_____

_____

Important Documents and Locations

Name:_____ Social Security #_____

Bank Account

Name of Bank_____

Address_____

Types of Accounts/Account No _____

_____

Safe Deposit Box Location:_____Location of keys_____

Other Accounts: Brokerage, Retirement, IRA, 401K

_____

_____

_____

_____

LOCATION OF

Birth Certificate_____

Children's Birth Certificates_____

Marriage Certificate_____

Deeds and Titles_____

Mortgages and Notes_____

Last Will and Testament_____

Military Discharge_____

Income tax records_____

Important Documents and Locations cont.

Insurance Policy Information

Company_____

Policy #_____

Name of Insured_____

Beneficiary_____

Veterans Benefits: ☐ YES   ☐ NO

Location of house keys_____

Safe combination etc._____

My Attorney is_____

Address_____City_____State____Zip_____

Phone_____

My Accountant is_____

Address_____City_____State____Zip_____

Phone_____

Additional Information

_____
_____
_____
_____
_____
_____

Digital Estate

In recent years the explosion of digital technology and social media has left most of us with a Digital Estate. That is, most of us have online accounts that need to be closed after our death or they will remain open long after we are gone. Criminals have started exploiting these digital remains to steal our identity even after we are deceased. I list here all online accounts with banks, retailers on and off-line and all social media outlets with my logon information and passwords so that you can close these accounts on my behalf.

Name	Web Address	LogIn ID	Password
(example) Recipe Direct	RecipeDirect.net	CaptTattoo	windward18

Additional Information or Comments

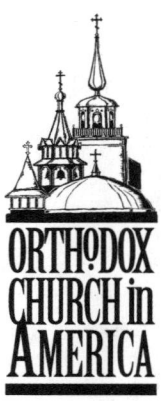

Bibliography

A Manual of Eastern Orthodox Prayers. Crestwood, NY: Saint Vladimir's Seminary Press, 1983.

Aphrahat, Saint. "Select Demonstrations." *Nicene and Post-Nicene Fathers, Volume 9*. Peabody, MA: Hendrickson, 1994.

Basil of Caesarea, Saint. "On the Spirit, Chapter XV." *Nicene and Post-Nicene Fathers, Volume 8*. Peabody, MA: Hendrickson, 1994.

———. "Letter VI (To the Wife of Nectarius)." *Nicene and Post-Nicene Fathers, Volume 8*. Peabody, MA: Hendrickson, 1994.

———. "Letter CL," *Nicene and Post-Nicene Fathers, Volume 8*. Peabody, MA: Hendrickson, 1994.

———. "Letter CVI (To the Soldier)," *Nicene and Post-Nicene Fathers, Volume 8*. Peabody, MA: Hendrickson, 1994.

———. "Letter CLI," *Nicene and Post-Nicene Fathers, Volume 8*. Peabody, MA: Hendrickson, 1994.

———. "Letter CCXXXVI (To the Same Amphilochius)," *Nicene and Post-Nicene Fathers, Volume 8*. Peabody, MA: Hendrickson, 1994.

———. "Letter CCLXIX (To the Wife of Arinthaus)," *Nicene and Post-Nicene Fathers, Volume 8*. Peabody, MA: Hendrickson, 1994.

Behr, John. *The Mystery of Christ, Life in Death*. Crestwood, NY: Saint Vladimir's Seminary Press, 2006.

Birkby, Robert C. *The Boy Scout Handbook*. Irving, TX: Boy Scouts of America, 1990.

Breck, John. *God With Us: Critical Issues in Christian Life and Faith*. Crestwood, NY: Saint Vladimir's Seminary Press, 2003.

———. *The Sacred Gift of Life: Orthodox Christianity and Bioethics*. Crestwood, NY: Saint Vladimir's Seminary Press, 1998.

Carlson, Lisa. *Caring for the Dead: Your Final Act of Love*. Hinesburg, VT: Upper Access Books, 1998.

Garvey, John. *Death and the Rest of Our Life*. Grand Rapids, MI: William B. Eerdman's Publishing Company, 2005.

Gregory of Nyssa, Saint. "On Infants' Early Deaths," *Nicene and Post-Nicene Fathers, Volume 5*. Peabody, MA: Hendrickson, 1994.

———. "On the Soul and Resurrection," *Nicene and Post-Nicene Fathers, Volume 5*. Peabody, MA: Hendrickson, 1994.

———. "Funeral Oration on Meletius," *Nicene and Post-Nicene Fathers, Volume 5*. Peabody, MA: Hendrickson, 1994.

———. "The Great Catechism," *Nicene and Post-Nicene Fathers, Volume 5*. Peabody, MA: Hendrickson, 1994.

Heinz, Donald. *The Last Passage: Recovering a Death of Our Own*. New York: Oxford University Press, 1999.

Hicks, Ralph. *Everyone Dies! Secrets That Can Save You Thousands in Unnecessary Funeral Costs*. Equitable Associates, LLC, 1999.

"*History of Embalming*." Wyoming Funeral Directors Association, January 27, 2002, http//www.wyfda.org/basics_3.htm.

Hopko, Thomas. *The Winter Pascha: Readings for the Christmas-Epiphany Season*. Crestwood, NY: Saint Vladimir's Seminary Press, 1997.

John Chrysostom, Saint. "Letter to a Young Widow," *Nicene and Post-Nicene Fathers, Volume 9*. Peabody, MA: Hendrickson, 1994.

———. "Concerning the Statues, Homily 2," *Nicene and Post-Nicene Fathers, Volume 9*. Peabody, MA: Hendrickson, 1994.

———. "Concerning the Statues, Homily 5," *Nicene and Post-Nicene Fathers, Volume 9*. Peabody, MA: Hendrickson, 1994.

———. "Concerning the Statues, Homily 7", *Nicene and Post-Nicene Fathers, Volume 9*. Peabody, MA: Hendrickson, 1994.

———. "Concerning the Statues, Homily 11," *Nicene and Post-Nicene Fathers, Volume 9*. Peabody, MA: Hendrickson, 1994.

———. "Concerning the Statues, Homily 15," *Nicene and Post-Nicene Fathers, Volume 9*. Peabody, MA: Hendrickson, 1994.

———. "Homily XLI on First Corinthians (1 Cor 15 35–36)," *Nicene and Post-Nicene Fathers, Volume 9*. Peabody, MA: Hendrickson, 1994.

———. "Homily LXII, On the Gospel of Saint John," *Nicene and Post-Nicene Fathers, Volume 14*. Peabody, MA: Hendrickson, 1994.

———. "Homily LXXVII, On the Gospel of Saint John," *Nicene and Post-Nicene Fathers, Volume 14*. Peabody, MA: Hendrickson, 1994.

———. "Homily LXXXVI, On the Gospel of Saint John," *Nicene and Post-Nicene Fathers, Volume 14*. Peabody, MA: Hendrickson, 1994.

———. "Homily XXXI, On the Gospel of Matthew," *Nicene and Post-Nicene Fathers, Volume 10*. Peabody, MA: Hendrickson, 1994.

John of Damascus, Saint. "An Exact Exposition of the Orthodox Faith," *Nicene and Post-Nicene Fathers, Volume 9*. Peabody, MA: Hendrickson, 1994.

Jones, Constance. *R.I.P. The Complete Book of Death and Dying*. The Stonesong Press, Inc., 1997.

Kyriakis, James. "Byzantine Burial Customs: Care of the Deceased from Death to the Prothesis." *The Greek Orthodox Theological Review*, Vol XIX, no.1, Spring 1974, p. 37.

Laderman, Gary. *Rest in Peace, A Cultural History of Death and the Funeral Home in Twentieth-Century America*. New York: Oxford University Press, 2003.

Lamm, Maurice. *The Jewish Way in Death and Mourning*, Middle Village, NY: Jonathan David Publishers, 1969.

Larchet, Jean-Claude. *The Theology of Illness*. Crestwood, NY: Saint Vladimir's Seminary Press, 2002.

Lawless, Julia. *The Illustrated Encyclopedia of Essential Oils*. London: Element, 1995.

Lossky, Vladimir. *The Mystical Theology of the Eastern Church*. Crestwood, NY: Saint Vladimir's Seminary Press, 1997.

Lyons, Jerri, and Janelle Va Melvin. *Final Passages: A Complete Home Funeral Guide*. Sebastopol, CA: Final Passages, 1999.

Mims, Cedric. *When We Die: The Science, Culture, and Rituals of Death*. St. Martin's Press, 1998.

Mitford, Jessica. *The American Way of Death Revisited*. New York: Alfred A. Knopf, 1998.

Mother Mary and Archimandrite Kallistos Ware, trans. *The Lenten Triodion*. South Canaan, PA: Saint Tikhon's Seminary Press, 2002.

Oden Thomas C., ed. *Ancient Christian Commentary on Scripture, New Testament Volume II, Mark*. Downers Grove, IL: Inter-Varsity Press, 1998.

Revised Standard Version of the Bible, with Apocrypha. New York: Oxford University Press, 2002.

Sagarin, Edward. *The Science and Art of Perfumery*. New York: McGraw-Hill, 1945.

Saint Athanasius Orthodox Academy, ed. *The Orthodox Study Bible*, Nashville: Thomas Nelson, 1993.

Schmemann, Alexander. *O Death, Where Is Thy Sting?* trans. Alexis Vinogradov, Crestwood, NY: Saint Vladimir's Seminary Press, 2003.

———. *The Liturgy of Death: Four Previously Unpublished Talks*. Yonkers, NY: Saint Vladimir's Seminary Press, 2016.

Schmidt, Alvin J. *Dust to Dust or Ashes to Ashes, A Biblical and Christian Examination of Cremation*. Salisbury, MA: Regina Orthodox Press Inc., 2005.

Sophrony, Archmandrite. *Saint Silouan the Athonite* trans. Rosemary Edmonds. Crestwood, NY: Saint Vladimir's Seminary Press, 1999.

Theophan the Recluse, Saint. *The Spiritual Life and How to Be Attuned to It* trans. A. Dockham. Saint Herman of Alaska Brotherhood, 1995.

———. *The Path to Salvation, A Manual of Spiritual Transformation* trans. Fr. Seraphim Rose. Saint Herman of Alaska Brotherhood, 1996.

Theophylact of Ochrid, Blessed. *The Explanation of the Holy Gospel According to Saint Mark* trans. Beck, Schaefer, and Kriegel. Chrysostom Press, House Springs, MO, 1993.

Vassiliadis, Nikolaos P. *The Mystery of Death* tr. Fr. Peter A. Chamberas. The Orthodox Brotherhood of Theologians "The Savior." 1997.

Ward, Benedicta, SLG, trans. *The Sayings of the Desert Fathers*. Kalamazoo, MI: Cistercian Publications, 1975.